Cambridge Elements ≡

Elements in Sign Languages
edited by
Erin Wilkinson
University of New Mexico
David Quinto-Pozos
University of Texas at Austin

TABOO IN SIGN LANGUAGES

Donna Jo Napoli
Swarthmore College
Jami Fisher
University of Pennsylvania
Gene Mirus
Gallaudet University

CAMBRIDGE
UNIVERSITY PRESS

Shaftesbury Road, Cambridge CB2 8EA, United Kingdom

One Liberty Plaza, 20th Floor, New York, NY 10006, USA

477 Williamstown Road, Port Melbourne, VIC 3207, Australia

314–321, 3rd Floor, Plot 3, Splendor Forum, Jasola District Centre,
New Delhi – 110025, India

103 Penang Road, #05–06/07, Visioncrest Commercial, Singapore 238467

Cambridge University Press is part of Cambridge University Press & Assessment,
a department of the University of Cambridge.

We share the University's mission to contribute to society through the pursuit of
education, learning and research at the highest international levels of excellence.

www.cambridge.org
Information on this title: www.cambridge.org/9781009291958

DOI: 10.1017/9781009291972

First published 2023

A catalogue record for this publication is available from the British Library

ISBN 978-1-009-29195-8 Paperback
ISSN 2752-9401 (online)
ISSN 2752-9398 (print)

Cambridge University Press & Assessment has no responsibility for the persistence
or accuracy of URLs for external or third-party internet websites referred to in this
publication and does not guarantee that any content on such websites is, or will
remain, accurate or appropriate.

Taboo in Sign Languages

Elements in Sign Languages

DOI: 10.1017/9781009291972
First published online: October 2023

Donna Jo Napoli
Swarthmore College

Jami Fisher
University of Pennsylvania

Gene Mirus
Gallaudet University

Author for correspondence: Donna Jo Napoli, dnapoli1@swarthmore.edu

Abstract: Taboo topics in deaf communities include the usual ones found in spoken languages, as well as ones particular to deaf experiences, both in how deaf people relate to hearing people and how deaf people interact with other deaf people. Attention to these topics can help linguists understand better the consequences of field method choices and lead them to adopt better ones. Taboo expressions in American Sign Language are innovative regarding the linguistic structures they play with. This creativity is evident across the grammar in non-taboo expressions, but seems to revel in profane ones. When it comes to the syntax, however, certain types of structures occur in taboo expressions that are all but absent elsewhere, showing grammatical possibilities that might have gone unnoticed without attention to taboo. Taboo expressions are innovative, as well, in how they respond to changing culture, where lexical items that are incoherent with community sensibilities are "corrected."

Keywords: sign language structure, morphology, syntax, sociolinguistics, creativity in language

ISBNs: 9781009291958 (PB), 9781009291972 (OC)
ISSNs: 2752-9401 (online), 2752-9398 (print)

Contents

1 Taboo

Taboo expressions are lexical items or larger constructions whose use in a given situation is strongly prohibited; they are considered rude or vulgar. Taboo speech consists of terms regarding religion, disease and death, sex, and bodily excretions (e.g., Montagu 1967). Studies of taboo speech have looked at general utility (Culpeper 2011), including exclamations, maledictions, and name-calling.

Societal behavior in a period of history may be reflected in taboo use. For example, in England the medieval period had a proliferation of religious profanities, seen in the words of only the crudest pilgrims in Chaucer's work; the Renaissance period inhibited such freedom, seen in the presence of only a scattering of profanities in Shakespeare's work; the Puritan Commonwealth strictly repressed behavior, witnessed in the biblical language of John Milton; the Restoration period was marked with extreme decadence, with the peppery language of Samuel Pepys; and so on (e.g., Hughes 2015). Taboo language can vary by sociolinguistic factors, including gender and, in bilinguals, primary language (e.g., Pilotti et al. 2012). And taboo language can help in studying historical linguistics. For example, among North Sea fishermen, it was taboo while at sea to mention the names of fish one was hoping to catch, for fear of scaring them away, or to mention the names of creatures one wanted to avoid, such as whales and certain birds, for fear of attracting them (Lockwood 1955). Taboo terms of this sort from the Norn language of Shetland fishermen persisted as a sort of secret language after the Norn language had fallen out of use, providing linguistic evidence for dating the shift from Norn to Scots (Knooihuizen 2008).

In recent years, studies have considered a wider range of issues regarding taboo language (Allan 2018). Many new studies focus on what taboo language teaches us about factors endemic to modernity, looking across media types (Azzaro 2018), comedy (Blake 2018), translation issues (Magazzù 2018), and how taboos in language reinforce culture (Van Oudenhoven et al. 2008) or control society (O'Driscoll 2020). The range of topics perceived as taboo in polite conversation has expanded in many communities today to include topics that can elicit strong differences of opinion, such as faith, politics, natural resources, consumerism, racial injustice, economic injustice, environmental injustice, climate change, child care, hair, meat consumption, gender identity, and so on.

In this Element, we examine properties of taboo expressions in American Sign Language (ASL) that offer information about linguistic structure and we alert readers to ethical behavior in studying the language of deaf communities (see Sections 1.3.4, 1.4.1, and 1.4.2). We expand upon our earlier work (Fisher, Mirus & Napoli 2018; Mirus, Fisher & Napoli 2020; Napoli, Fisher & Mirus 2013), here organized to help deliver a more holistic picture of sign taboo.

1.1 Background: Taboo Expressions Are Special

Taboo expressions and taboo topics of conversation differ from taboo acts (incest, murder, bestiality, pederasty, etc.) in that whether these expressions or topics are, in fact, taboo, depends very much on the conversational context. In a discussion with a rabbi, psychiatrist, proctologist, lover, and so on, the use of lexical items related to otherwise taboo topics may be perfectly acceptable. And when bonds of friendship are ensured, discussion may be riddled with taboo expressions, where neither the person using the taboo nor the person witnessing the taboo think about offense at all (Tierney 2017); to the contrary, this use of taboo often signals in-group membership (Cho & Tian 2020).

Studies in neurobiology support the thesis that taboo expressions are special. Discussing a taboo topic in euphemistic language has different effects on the brain from discussing it using taboo expressions (Hansen, McMahon & de Zubicaray 2019). Aphasic patients can preserve taboo expressions when other types of expressions elude them (van Lancker & Cummings 1999). Frontal lobe damage increases swearing frequency while amygdala damage decreases it (Jay 2009). And taboo-expression effects are evident in the Stroop task (Song et al. 2017).

Studies in linguistics confirm that taboo expressions are special. The recent work of many linguists, examining many languages, shows that taboo expressions present unusual morphological and syntactic behavior in spoken language (Napoli & Hoeksema 2009), leading to insights into grammar that are not so easily gained otherwise. Typically, the enlistment of lexical items by constructions is based on their category and features, which in turn are in part determined by lexical semantics. However, in these taboo constructions, lexical meaning plays no role. Thus, theories of grammar that rely on a compositional semantics cannot adequately account for the distribution of taboo terms across the grammar and need to be modified to include whole meaningful constructions (Hoeksema & Napoli 2008).

Taboo constructions (fixed constructions containing taboo terms) in many languages can be used as emphasis markers regardless of literal meaning (*Why the fuck did you do that?*). Additionally, they can be used as resultatives that intensify (*Smith studied his balls off*). What matters is not the sense of the words *fuck* or *balls*, but their taboo nature – a culturally motivated pragmatic status. Taboo language is also used in ASL for emphasis and in resultative intensifiers, but differently from English.

1.2 Taboo and Sign Languages

The linguistic specialness of taboo expressions in ASL and in any other sign languages is largely underexamined. Among the few linguistic works on sign taboo is a study of the offensiveness of sexual orientation terminology in ASL (Rudner & Butowsky 1981) and a study of how members of the Venezuelan deaf community deal with vulgarity in terminology regarding death and intercourse (Pietrosemoli 1994). We refer to recent works that focus on the relationship of phonological parameters to taboo in a few other sign languages. Nevertheless, our familiarity with several sign languages leads us to suspect that many of the creative techniques of ASL pointed out here may be common among sign languages.

Several caveats are needed. Unsurprisingly, many taboo expressions in spoken languages have equally taboo counterparts in sign languages. And in both spoken and sign languages, a given taboo expression can be used in multiple ways, depending on context. Throughout the present work, we try to give a single appropriate context for the taboo signs we discuss, but we are not suggesting that this is the only or even the most common (type of) context.

Additionally, while taboo terms are recognized by those within a given community, there can be disagreement as to whether a term is offensive or merely blunt, whether in spoken languages (Burridge 2012: 66) or sign languages (Sze, Wei & Wong 2017: 194 ff). Here we use the sensibilities of our deaf consultants as a guide. In this regard, one must pay close attention to facial articulations. Facial expression is a crucial part of sign, carrying grammatical, lexical, and affective information (Liddell 2003); facial articulations of many types can occur alone as taboo insults and can make an otherwise inoffensive sentence taboo.

While there are many commonalities between (studying) taboos in spoken and sign languages, there are also differences. Describing a person based on visually obvious characteristics, including unflattering properties (a large nose, acned skin) and sexual properties (ample breasts, curvy buttocks) can be considered taboo among hearing people, depending on culture and times, but is not taboo among deaf people (Mindess 2006). This is acceptable behavior, neither rude nor politically incorrect.

On the other hand, some taboo terms in sign languages do not have counterparts in spoken languages due to experiences common to deaf people that are not shared by hearing people, and to complexities within deaf communities (Leigh, Andrews & Harris 2016). Among such common experiences are the obstacles that deaf people encounter in acquiring/learning language. Further, there are details about the American context that may be unique. In the spirit of respect for people and customs in deaf communities and service to our field, we cautiously but frankly mire ourselves in a rudimentary overview of taboo behaviors regarding deaf people in a hearing world and deaf people within deaf communities. It is within this complex framework of confusions and privileges that the varieties of taboos we address in later sections have arisen. We will see that, just as the study of taboo expressions in spoken languages can lead to insights about linguistic theory and about particular language grammars, so can the study of taboo expressions in sign languages. However, different sorts of insights emerge.

1.3 Deaf People in a Hearing-Dominated World

Language is a staggeringly important cognitive activity. Language allows us to gain information beyond what our somatosensory system can access. Language is our most reliable way to convey our thoughts to others and to appreciate others' thoughts, our major means of cooperating with each other, and a crucial player in making friends, falling in love, telling jokes, partaking of humanity.

Many hearing people might never explicitly consider nor appreciate the fact that they participate in language – it's a given. But most deaf people do. People in deaf communities have highly varied linguistic experiences and abilities. Often, many years of frustration are spent learning to vocalize while being denied sign. Accordingly, sign is dear to deaf people in a way that is hard for most hearing people to comprehend at first. If a deaf child grows up in a signing environment, that child acquires language naturally – no heroes required – just as happens with a hearing child in a speaking or signing environment. But nearly 96 percent of deaf children in the USA are born into hearing families (Mitchell & Karchmer 2004), and it takes heroic efforts for those children to acquire language. Most hearing parents are not initially provided with adequate resources for learning a sign language, and efforts to deter hearing parents from teaching their deaf children to sign are pervasive and coordinated (Mauldin 2016). In developed countries the majority of deaf newborns are given a cochlear implant within the first two years of life. Many hearing families raise their implanted child strictly orally, on the advice of medical professionals (Humphries et al. 2017). The human brain did not evolve to interpret cochlear implant signals as language, so implanted children must be trained (long hours daily, for years) in order to have a chance at distinguishing language among those signals. Many do not succeed, despite diligent training. Once the family realizes that the child is not developing linguistically as hoped, they turn to sign, often after the period when the child's brain is most plastic and ready to acquire language (Humphries et al. 2012). At this point, families learn to sign (to varying degrees) and, hopefully, bring their deaf children to events with good signing models. The children are, however, latecomers to language, and the architecture of the brain is affected by early linguistic deprivation (Pénicaud et al. 2013). Hence, nearly all deaf people are hyper-aware of language itself as a privilege.

This rudimentary background on language acquisition can help us to understand language behaviors by hearing people that are considered taboo by deaf people, and why they are taboo. Topics in this subsection center on the interface of deaf and hearing people with attention to effects of power dynamics, including oppression and marginalization of deaf people by hearing people. While the matters we discuss are pertinent to the situation of signers in a world where the majority hears and speaks, our observations allow for analogies to other oppressed linguistic communities. As such, they may alert scholars to possibilities of taboos specific to the nature of the oppression.

1.3.1 Linguistic and Cultural Appropriation

When a hearing person learns to speak a second language, such as an English speaker learning Japanese, the situations in which they use Japanese are limited; unless they find themselves with a Japanese speaker or go to Japan, they are unlikely to speak Japanese outside the L2 classroom. The chances of them assuming the role of teaching Japanese to others are low unless they explicitly train for that. They might think of telling a Japanese person that the pronunciation of the word they had learned was different from that of the Japanese speaker, but they would never suggest that the Japanese speaker might be wrong. And it is ludicrous to think that they might present themselves as an authority on Japanese haiku or traditional Japanese Kabuki or Noh theater or even on contemporary Japanese rap without extensive study.

Not so when a hearing person learns to sign. Students of sign often communicate to varying degrees in sign outside of the L2 classroom, often instructed by their teachers to do so, and they do it in public. Signing has advantages spoken languages lack – communicating without others noticing, across a room, in a quiet space, with taboo messages without fear of reprisal, and so on (and both hearing and deaf members of village sign languages reap these utilitarian benefits; see Croce 1985). New signers often feel empowered quickly, even though ASL students are only moderately good at assessing their own competence in signing (Stauffer 2012). That empowerment leads them to behaviours discussed in this paragraph, raising the hackles of deaf people.

An ASL student teaching another hearing person how to sign something – sometimes incorrectly – is commonplace. Often ASL students do this in front of deaf signers, looking for congratulations on what amounts to garbled signing. If they do not know a sign, they might make one up. And, while signs are coined largely using iconicity, so many different factors are at play that the lexicons of different sign languages are not predictable nor mutually intelligible, so these guesses are often wrong. No one would simply make up a word in Japanese (or any other spoken language) if they didn't know the correct word (unless they were engaging in what Hill [2014: 198] calls "elite racist discourse"). Annoying!

But perhaps not as annoying as one of the most common taboos: telling a deaf person, "That's not how I was taught to make that sign," and then proceeding to make the sign as if the deaf person should receive it with interest, if not gratitude. Imagine telling a speaker from Tokyo that you pronounce the word *arigato* differently from how she pronounces it. She might write you off as a fool, but would probably not be offended. But doing the same to a deaf person is sharply offensive; it is a reminder that a deaf person's linguistic legitimacy has historically been, and still is, scrutinized, challenged, and suppressed by hearing people.

But hearing people sometimes go beyond gaffes. Learning a second language can give the sense that one has a different identity in that other language, and that can be thrilling (Wilson 2013). Students of ASL can fall in love with this new signing world and their new self in it, and they can appropriate deaf-community tendencies in a stinging way. This appropriation is common on the Internet, where many hearing people have chosen to perform a sign version of a song. While some say they do it with the hopes of conveying the beauty of signing, they miss the point that signing is not a form of performance art, but real language (Solomon & Miller 2014). They wouldn't perform a song in Spanish before an audience unless they were fluent or properly trained (such as an opera singer), so why do this in sign? They misrepresent and, at times, fetishize the language, and the frustrating – infuriating? – part is that their hearing audience doesn't know that. While we might laugh at someone who sings a song in Spanish with a grating American accent, we might admire and mimic someone who signs a song in ASL with who-knows-what kind of pronunciation.

Another case of linguistic and cultural appropriation is when a nonfluent signer from outside deaf communities uses signing for self-promotion and profit. Cherry-picking language and presenting oneself as a teacher-expert are taboo, particularly when that language is of an oppressed minority community that one is not a member of. The YouTube account known as Dirty Signs with Kristin teaches obscene signs that are often inaccurate, and comes off as derogatory and exploitative of deaf people (Powell 2012). In 2012, the creator published a book of obscene signs, financially profiting from her inappropriate behavior. Public outcry from deaf communities arose (Permenter 2012; TrueBizMe 2012). In contrast, there are recent videos of deaf people demonstrating and explaining profanities, giving their own perspectives on and examples of taboo signs they see and use daily (e.g., Taylor 2017). These authentic, deaf-community insights reveal taboo without exploitation.

The Internet has a well-known disinhibiting effect, and it can exacerbate the fact that language and topics that are taboo in one's own linguistic community can seem less taboo in another language, as though the other language somehow exempts us from shame or embarrassment (Gawinkowska, Paradowski & Bilewicz 2013). Finally, interest in the obscenities of other languages is high. Nevertheless, when it comes to sign, something goes beyond these general tendencies. Perhaps the highly visual nature of sign languages creates an allure – a voyeuristic relish in the graphic nature of taboo. This is where offense comes in: dirty signs, like off-color jokes and jokes that deal with a community's prejudices, are in poor taste, and that poor taste belongs to the community, not to outsiders who might not understand the way they are intended. The Internet has been a tremendously useful tool for deaf communities. But it has also been a tool of exposure and marginalization (Saunders 2016), stomping further and harder on an oppressed minority.

1.3.2 Issues Involving Identity

In a conversation involving deaf people it is important to reveal auditory status immediately. A hearing person who enters a sign conversation and is taken to be deaf but later discovered to be hearing can engender a sense of violation. That hearing person was putting themself in the position of potentially taking part in in-group behavior – critical to the identity of the deaf conversants (Tropp & Wright 2001). Further, a hearing person who allows themself to be taken as deaf can be perceived as taking unfair advantage of being able to sign – a deaf person cannot pretend to be hearing, after all (Bat-Chava 1994).

Signing and deaf-community tendencies have become so popular that we now find deaf groupies and wannabes (e.g., Deaf-Wannabee, founded in 2000). The interlopers are hearing who adopt deaf ways and sometimes have even mutilated themselves to lose their hearing (Veale 2006). Deaf wannabes are recognized as having a pathology that the medical profession needs to find a coherent way to deal with (Davey & Phillips 2013).

The idea that hearing people would want to become deaf can offend. Deaf people, particularly those with hearing aids or cochlear implant, work hard in a hearing environment, straining to understand a minimal amount. Other deaf people are excluded in hearing environments. Choosing to deafen oneself is tantamount to a slap in the face for deaf people, who would love to have the chance to relax with the effortless access to speech hearing people have. This is not to say that deaf people do not appreciate being deaf. Many do, and they explain to others the benefits of Deafhood (see Lentz [2014] and other videos done for the Deafhood Foundation or independently). As I. King Jordan, former President of Gallaudet University, answered in 1990 when he was asked if he'd rather be hearing, "That's almost like asking a black person if he would rather be white . . . I don't think of myself as missing something or as incomplete. . . . It's a common fallacy if you don't know deaf people or deaf issues. You think it's a limitation" (Fine & Fine 1990). That said, deaf people do not proselytize for deafness. Rather, the idea is that a healthy identity involves accepting oneself, embracing one's experiences. Deaf groupies and wannabes do not ingratiate themselves with deaf communities. Further, there are hearing people new to the whole idea of deaf communities who police the boundaries of deaf identity more fiercely than deaf people do. They want to toe the line so much that they wind up excluding many deaf people based on arbitrary notions of deaf ideals.

Another identity matter relevant to our discussion arises with the terms *disability*, *disabled*, *handicap*, and the like. Not all functional diversity is viewed the same way by everyone, even among communities of people labeled disabled (e.g., Deal 2003). Further, today people are moving away from a dysfunctional model toward a diversity model with respect to (nearly) every-thing previously gathered under the disability aegis. But that movement is old hat for deaf communities. For decades many deaf people have proclaimed that deafness is an auditory status, not a disability (Lane 2002). In places where the incidence of deafness is high (as with village sign languages), being deaf is simply a trait a person has, like hair color or height (Lane, Pillard & French 2000). Deaf people cannot hear; beyond that, deaf eople have the same range of abilities hearing people have. This sentiment is memorialized in the two-sign phrase DEAF CAN, which is the name of a nonprofit organization that provides services to deaf people. Deaf people are represented across the professions, where many are famous (Start ASL 2008–17). Other deaf people are living without fame in satisfaction and success (Longmore & Umansky 2001). The areas in which they find satisfaction and success can surprise hearing people (including music and dance).

More recently, deaf communities have faced the criticism that the distancing of deaf people from disabled people may be one more way of supporting society's ableist structures (Kersten-Parrish 2021). Many groups have been denied a seat at the table, and it is imperative that deaf communities join with other oppressed groups to secure the kind of cross-systems changes necessary for meaningful progress (as in educational matters; Cruz, Firestone & Love 2023).

In fact, despite the rhetoric, deaf people have realized this all along; they are quick to note their rights under the Americans with Disabilities Act of 1990, calling for an interpreter when the situation demands. Deaf people recognize that situations can cut off their ability to communicate, thus situationally disabling them. This is one of those instances in which the purpose of using the label determines whether it is taboo.

One issue of identity involves the signs that a signing hearing person knows. Place names are a telling example. In an introductory ASL course, one learns sign names for some countries and cities, but also for local towns and institutions. The local deaf school is of primary importance to the deaf community. Cities with influential deaf schools and deaf institutions are as central to knowledge about deaf life in America as New York, Los Angeles, and Miami are to knowledge about hearing life. If you don't learn these important place names, and, worse, if you are an interpreter and you don't learn them, you disrespect the community (Suggs 2012).

Some hearing people who become hard-of-hearing refuse to wear a hearing aid, insisting that everyone speak loudly or simply not understanding the language around them. This behavior can be taken as an affront, as though being identified as deaf is so awful that it's better to give up access to communication. Deaf people are not wrong to see such behavior as suspect; in America, only 14 percent of people over the age of fifty with hearing loss use a hearing aid – because "hearing aids still carry a stigma" (Seliger 2012).

Hearing people often take months or years of knowing each other before they reveal their history. Deaf signers, instead, learn a lot about each other at a first meeting – where they were born, raised, educated, their family situation, whether this is their third marriage, and how they feel about the new president (Swinbourne 2013). When a deaf person opens up to a hearing person and there is no reciprocity, it can seem like hearing people cast aspersions on the deaf way of relating.

While being receptive to overtures of friendship matters, it's important to understand propriety. In this regard, sign interactions can come across as more forthright about sexual matters and bodily functions than spoken interactions because of the visually explicit nature of signing. But, in fact, the range of attitudes toward sexual matters and the sense of privacy about bodily functions vary among deaf people as among hearing people. So, hearing people can feel they have more of an intimacy with a deaf person than in fact they do, and they can, in turn, behave inappropriately.

Another taboo offense is to make assumptions based solely on the fact that someone is deaf. Just as not all sign languages are the same, not all deaf people are – intellectually, politically, or otherwise. Most of all, not all deaf people sign and not all deaf people want to help hearing people practice their signing.

1.3.3 Hearing Privilege

Hearing privilege affects deaf communities and deaf–hearing interactions. Intentional use of this privilege is oppressive and taboo. If you are in a sign conversation and a hearing person comes along, it is taboo to talk with that third person without including the deaf person. Some deaf people find simultaneous communication (signing and speaking at the same time) an acceptable way to be included. This taboo is interesting linguistically because if an Italian friend passed by and you spoke Italian, you might turn away from a hearing person you were speaking English with to talk briefly in Italian without bothering to translate into English. What makes the situation with a deaf person different is the role of privilege. A hearing person could, in principle, learn any spoken language, but a deaf person is excluded from accessing spoken language. Thus, the hearing person in this scenario has a privilege – and power to choose to include or exclude the deaf person.

Another privilege that hearing people enjoy is incidental information. Hearing people are bombarded with informative content via speech, whether or not directed at them and whether or not they put effort into listening. In contrast, deaf people are not bombarded with information via sign. Instead, deaf people frequently find themselves in contexts where the norm is speech. Following one stream of information without a sign language mediator expends significant effort and is quickly tiring with little informational reward. Attending to multiple streams is disorienting and likely counter-productive. Hearing people have the privilege of skipping from conversation stream to conversation stream; instead, deaf people in a hearing context would need a nonverbal cue that another conversation might be of interest to attend to. This goes for signing deaf people as well as implanted deaf people; too much spoken information overloads the interlocutor and minimizes access. Turn taking and attention to visual cues is deeply ingrained into conversational habits of deaf communities.

Even in a signing environment, deaf people must actively attend in order to glean information. A hearing person can turn their back on a speaker or shut their eyes and still get information; a deaf person cannot. This difference in attention demands is recognized in the literature on educating deaf children (Gregory 1998) and on the quotidian medical knowledge adults have (Job

2004). When a deaf person misses out on an event everyone else knew about because the information was passed in a way that excluded them, it might be oversight; if a hearing person does this to a deaf friend (or employee) repeatedly, that's bitter.

Correcting a deaf person's pronunciation of a word they have voiced can also be taboo. If the deaf person hasn't asked for such feedback, it shouldn't be given, as it suggests that perfect speech is more important than message content. It also signals that the hearing person has more power and spoken language has more value in the conversational dyad.

Breaking eye contact while talking to a deaf person, whether speaking or signing, is rude. It's not just part of deaf interaction to make eye contact, it's crucial to a deaf person's understanding of the conversation. If a person in the conversation looks away, that action indicates usurpation of conversational power. If a person turns their head away, that cuts off intelligibility.

1.3.4 Exploitation

There is a long history of exploitation of deaf people for hearing benefit. Repeated and continued incidences of exploitation have resulted in a heightened awareness of hearing people's motivations. We highlight certain types of scenarios to bring awareness to inherent and uneven power dynamics that risk exploitation of deaf people.

Many hearing professionals gain financial advantage or professional advancement through interaction with deaf communities, including audiologists, interpreters, linguists, and teachers for the deaf. The relationship between deaf communities and these groups is complex. On the one hand, they may rely on them – particularly interpreters and teachers. On the other hand, they may feel resentment at being under their control. When interpreters try to coin signs or impose their own ways of rendering a deaf person's message, deaf people can feel oppressed by the very people who are supposed to be serving them (Baker-Shenk 1986). When interpreters get the spotlight for creative signing instead of the deaf people from whom the signs originated, ire rises in deaf communities (Zola 2015). Then there are those who study the community, and walk away with a publication that promotes their career and never return to that community; this smacks of exploitation.

Since our audience here is mostly linguists, we mention a number of deaf-friendly behaviors to adopt in doing linguistic analysis (Singleton et al. 2015). Not adopting these behaviors is unethical and taboo. Deaf communities should be regarded as hosts, and involved in every aspect of the project (Harris, Holmes & Mertens 2009). Deaf participants in the research should be fully informed of their rights in their preferred method of communication, rather than asking them to read a consent form (Singleton, Jones & Hanumantha 2014). Researchers should be aware of potential insecurities (linguistic and otherwise) of deaf consultants and be careful not to enter into a power relationship fed by those insecurities. Researchers should give back to the community via disseminating results in accessible materials – sign and print. Participants should be acknowledged in the work and remunerated.

1.4 Deaf People within Deaf Communities

Only in the past sixty years, following the ground-breaking work of William Stokoe, have linguists come to understand that sign languages are bona fide languages (for the impact of Stokoe, see Hochgesang & Miller 2016). In fact, only within that period have deaf people themselves come to understand that (Battison 2013). But the road leading to this understanding has been bumpy; as a result, deaf people have had a wide range of relationships with and attitudes toward sign languages (Leigh 2009), though in many places today sign language communities express pride in their language and embrace sign stories and poetry as bona fide literature (Bauman, Nelson & Rose 2006).

In this subsection we look at language behaviors and interactions among deaf people that can cause offense, which largely involve social hierarchies. The deaf community is characterized by camaraderie. This is not surprising since many deaf people find in deaf communities important things denied them at home; deaf community is a kind of surrogate family (Solomon 2012). About 90 percent of deaf marry other deaf (Schein 1989). Deaf communities present themselves to outsiders (hearing) as a united front. That means that discussing hierarchy within these communities is walking in taboo territory – a minefield. We do not intend our discussion of discord within deaf communities as a gratuitous assault on that united front. We do this with respect for the communities and with an eye toward furthering knowledge of taboo in general and toward improving (by expansion) the corpora that linguists consider when analyzing sign languages. Deaf communities are complex and their heterogeneity means that the possibilities for offending are multiple, so work like ours has no chance of being comprehensive. We hope others will follow up with refinements.

We discuss diversity within deaf communities, where the collective experience of navigating a predominantly hearing world is often central to connecting with other community members. Intuitively, these connections center on the use of sign languages, but those deaf people who do not sign have commonalities with deaf people who do. People in deaf communities often seek each other out for social purposes but also political ones. They rally around language rights and against discrimination, working toward parity of access and respect for deaf people. More recently, deaf communities have become more open to non-signers, forming alliances to further common goals.

All this is pertinent to linguistics. Often linguists gather data from a small contingent of a community, the educationally elite. Data from different contingents might lead to results with different implications for linguistic theory. Linguists tend to see those data in spoken languages as falling within the purview of sociolinguistics. But in deaf communities those data might be more representative of the majority of signers.

1.4.1 Hierarchies and Tension within Deaf Communities: the American Context

Identity politics within deaf communities are largely a matter of a linguistic model being superimposed from the outside. Though we do not wish to referee boundaries and hierarchies within the larger deaf community, we examine identity politics in the American scene here so that our international reader, in particular, might better understand the examples in the following sections.

As early as 1976, a detailed study of the communication network among deaf people in America concluded "not only that the deaf are increasingly leading and managing their own affairs but also that those deaf from birth or infancy, those with deaf parents, and those who began signing with others early in life are emerging as leaders in this society" (Stokoe, Bernard & Padden 1976: 208). This makes sense in that the celebration of sign language is an affirmation of deaf identity (Lane 2005); these deaf leaders have the most confirmed deaf identities. The deaf elite are, by and large, deaf-of-deaf, well-educated (college degree), hold middle-class or better jobs, and participate in local and national associations for deaf advocacy and outreach (Holcomb 2013). They are distinguished from oral deaf, from deaf people who did not have a chance to learn to sign (well), and from grassroots deaf (Burdiss 2016, in which the term has been part of discussions of deaf advocacy for decades; see Hudnall 1976), who occupy a different social stratum and wield less power within deaf communities. The deaf elite were the leaders of the successful Deaf President Now! Movement of 1988 that led to I. King Jordan being appointed the first deaf president of Gallaudet University (Kensicki 2001). Within Gallaudet, members of the deaf elite can be found at all institutional levels, including fraternities that tacitly accept only members of their own elite status. Historically, employment also gave a deaf person stature; being seen as valuable by hearing people and having an income confirmed one's worth. Deaf mendicants were decried as vagrants by organizations such as the National Fraternal Society for the Deaf (Burch 2004).

From 1880 in Milan, Italy, when hearing educators decreed that education of deaf people must follow an oralist methodology, spoken language and manually encoded forms became the norm in educational settings. One example was the Rochester Method, wherein deaf students were educated through the finger-spelled alphabet to promote print literacy; other signing was disallowed (Musselman 2000). Print literacy opens opportunities in mainstream society and allows social and economic opportunities; the lack of print literacy exposed one to accusations of being mentally feeble (Burch & Joyner 2007).

Low in the hierarchy are grassroots deaf, who often have not had an opportunity to go to college and do not travel much. In some communities, grassroots and deaf elite socialize together, and in others, they do not (Holcomb 2013). Some claim that grassroots deaf are the "true carriers of ASL" (Krieger 2007). Grassroots deaf network among one another and tend to be close-knit. Recently, grassroots deaf have joined together to gain greater visibility in fighting discrimination, and improving economic potential and communication access (Burdiss 2016).

These demarcations of a deaf elite seem to be a relatively new and American phenomenon. We hypothesize that linguists had their part in this: over the past nearly sixty years in sign language linguistics, researchers have prioritized deaf-of-deaf experiences for linguistic authenticity. Such priorities may have created a notion of superiority of the deaf-of-deaf experience within deaf communities. The reality that the deaf-of-deaf are statistically fewer than 5 percent of the deaf community makes the possibility of being part of this elite miniscule and likely reinforces the elite status.

1.4.2 Auditory Status, Facility with Signing, and Cochlear Implants

Some deaf children are born into deaf families and begin acquiring sign from birth. Likewise, hearing children born into deaf families may acquire sign from birth. Often, a deaf child in a hearing family can have a hearing younger sibling. That younger sibling might acquire both a spoken language and a sign language from birth. Thus, there are native signers who are deaf and native signers who are hearing. However, nearly all deaf children are the only deaf people in their family. They might have well-informed parents who immediately start learning to sign and bring them into contact with signing deaf people. Or they might not. Some of these deaf people learn to sign early and some later. If a child receives a cochlear implant and the family follows a zero-tolerance-to-alternative-approaches protocol, that child might not be introduced to sign until much later – as an adolescent or adult.

This mixed situation raises issues for linguists gathering data. Some have taken the position that a linguistic consultant must be at least a second-generation, deaf-of-deaf signer (Petitto et al. 2000). Generally, this is the position taken by those doing studies of the architecture of the brain. Others, particularly those more interested in grammar, have taken the position that exposure to sign by the age of three, ability to judge a sentence's grammaticality with ease, and daily contact with the deaf community for more than ten years together assure a consultant's reliability (Mathur & Rathmann 2006). Still others, perhaps at a loss for finding enough deaf signers with those prerequisites, gather data from all signers, listing such characteristics as hearing status, family hearing status, age when first exposed to a sign language, and length of exposure to a sign language, and then see whether those with certain characteristics on that list turn out to give different data from the others, allowing one or more of these characteristics to be singled out as relevant for defining competence with respect to the particular matters investigated (Costello, Fernández & Landa 2006). In studies that are more about usage of language, even that list of characteristics might not play a role. Rather, deaf people for whom signing is their primary and preferred mode of communication might serve perfectly well (Napoli & Mirus 2015).

All of this ties into our discussion of taboo because the questions linguists ask about language exposure raise, once more, the specter of not being an adequate signer – and, therefore, often of not being linguistically adequate period. The questions themselves can shake a deaf person's confidence in their identity. They must be posed in culturally sensitive ways. Indeed, in some deaf communities it is simply not accepted protocol for scholars to ask such questions; a person's self-declared membership in the deaf community is enough to include them in the study (Napoli, Sutton-Spence & Quadros 2017).

1.4.3 Subgroups That Comprise Deaf Communities in America

We now touch on some of the subgroups of American deaf communities. While we intend to be inclusive, we recognize that with so many varied deaf experiences, it is not possible to account for the exact experience of all deaf people, so we focus on subgroups that are linguistically based.

The most marginalized group is oral deaf. They are sometimes accused of being hearing wannabes and, at the same time, deaf wannabes (Horejes 2012). They are sometimes rural deaf people without the opportunity to learn sign due to lack of models or they were born to families who chose not to expose their children to sign so they could integrate as much as possible into the hearing world. Though sentiments within American deaf communities are changing to become more accepting of nonsigning deaf people, nonsigning deaf people have historically been pushed to the periphery, sometimes mocked and often excluded. The name sign for the Clarke Schools for Hearing and Speech is an insult sign that pokes fun at the strictly oral philosophy and practice of the school and its students. Perhaps even more marked within deaf communities are oral deaf with cochlear implants; they not only do not sign, they may be visually identified by surgery scars (Hollins 2000).

There are extremely diverse representations of hearing levels within deaf communities, but ability to sign is crucial to social acceptance. Hard-of-hearing people who sign have a better chance of being accepted somewhat (Davis 2002), while hard-of-hearing people who do not are often treated as outsiders (Rush 2014). With sign ability as an indicator of being in or out, being in-between can amount to being stuck between two worlds with no comfortable fit.

Alison Aubrecht, a mental health counselor at Michigan School for the Deaf, was raised in a hearing family and mainstreamed in school. In an interview (Eckhardt 2002) Aubrecht talks about growing up with the sense that she didn't belong anywhere and how difficult it was to find herself deemed an outsider by deaf people. She offers outreach videos on the Internet for people who feel anguish caused by language access and matters of fluency (Aubrecht 2017).

Yet this whole seemingly linguistically based hierarchy is clouded by the fact that hearing children of deaf adults (CODAs) have access to sign, but are not among the elite even though they are commonly as competent linguistically as deaf-of-deaf and often self-identify as part of deaf communities (Miller 2004). CODAs are intimate viewers of deaf communities, but they have not suffered the same oppression; they enjoy the hearing privilege that deaf people are not afforded. For some, this can preclude them from deaf communities (Davis 2007) or relegate their membership as peripheral (Bishop & Hicks 2005). Being insiders and outsiders at the same time, CODAs have unique needs and have had their own international organization since 1983 that serves as a forum for sharing CODA experiences (Children of Deaf Adults, Inc.; Brother 2017). They are linguistically complex – often using a sign language natively, the ambient spoken language natively (although some experience a bumpy start), and even commonly a blend of the two in CODA-talk (Preston 1994). But they are of-deaf, not deaf-of-deaf, which makes their ultimate position within deaf communities less central than they may personally feel, as they've been a part of this world from birth.

Nevertheless, and at odds with this picture, there are ways in which elitism within American deaf communities is defined in terms of being more like hearing people (i.e., audism; Humphries 1977). Education, particularly English-language literacy, has been an important factor in attaining elite status since the beginnings of American deaf communities (Robinson 2010). The notion of spoken language superiority was so deeply internalized that even deaf-of-deaf believed that signing with an English influence was more refined than ASL (see Benjamin Bahan's anecdote in the film *Through Deaf Eyes* in Hott 2007: 59:09–1:00:24).

1.4.4 Gender and Race Diversity within Deaf Communities

While deaf-of-deaf and fluently signing deaf people are the elite within some American deaf communities, this status is truest for white males (Robinson 2010, 2012). As Burch and Sutherland (2006: 141) say, despite the unified front to the outside world, many factors such as "race, class, gender, and disability caused considerable fissures within the Deaf-World." Until recently, the specific lived experiences of these groups have been overshadowed by white male deaf experiences. In the spirit of working toward inclusive deaf studies, we briefly highlight subgroups of the larger deaf community that have historically been marginalized from without and within.

The interface of the many allegiances deaf people have informs the nuanced identities of individuals as they relate to one another and to society (Crenshaw 1989). While we focus here on specific subgroups, deaf people do not experience life in such discrete terms; every deaf person's identity is informed by their personal journey.

Past attitudes toward women in America led to appreciation of them as physical but not intellectual beings (Brueggemann & Burch 2006), resulting in deaf women's social and economic statuses lagging behind that of deaf men (Sheridan 2001), but outreach organizations such as Deaf Women United (2016) work to mitigate such disparities, which have in fact been diminishing (Garberoglio et al. 2021). In some other countries the situation has been worse; in Japan, for example, many deaf women had forced sterilizations and were "not allowed to express themselves" until the Deaf Women's Movement, led by Riuko Oikawa beginning in the 1970s (Kobayashi & Osugi 2020). With regard to effects of gender on language, we find in Ireland, for example, several differences between male and female signing due to the fact that deaf children were educated in schools run by the Dominican Sisters and Sisters of Mercy, which were gender segregated until recently (O'Connell 2016).

Black deaf communities in America have been delineated by linguistic and educational terms for decades. Racial segregation in the south led to black deaf schools (Aramburo 1994), with black varieties of ASL (McCaskill et al. 2011), some not mutually intelligible with white ASL (such as Raleigh Signs). Black varieties of ASL and their signers were looked down on by white deaf people.

Gallaudet University did not admit black students until the 1950s (Hairston & Smith 1983). Racially segregated deaf clubs persisted for years (Padden & Humphries 1988). In wasn't until spring of 2023 that the Center for Black Studies at Gallaudet University held its first symposium to introduce the emerging field of Black Deaf Studies, with attention to education, linguistics, culture, and rights in a global setting.

Academic studies of other racial groups within deaf communities are even fewer and information on linguistic differences is scarce (Garberoglio et al. 2021) but the work dispels the myth that there is one deaf community of people who discard all identities beyond deaf.

There are also resonances of ableism in deaf communities. DeafBlind and DeafDisabled have historically been excluded as a rhetorical strategy to challenge social constructions of deafness as disability (Fox 1880). This attitude "shaped deaf activism throughout the twentieth century" (Robinson 2010: 17–18). Choosing only one aspect – deafness – of a complex, interconnected, functionally diverse identity serves to minimize what is essential to individual deaf experiences (Burke 2013). Interest in, and studies of, tactile sign, however, have increased dramatically (for the USA, Edwards 2014, 2018, 2022; for the Netherlands, Janssen, Riksen-Walraven & van Dijk 2002; for Sweden, Mesch 2000; Mesch & Raanes 2023), and recently there is a deliberate effort to be inclusive of deaf people from all backgrounds and with a range of functional diversities (Bauman 2009), though that end is far from realized.

2 Data Gathering

The data discussed in the following sections were gathered for earlier studies of ours. Those papers give copious citations, which we cannot offer here. Instead, we apologize and try to limit ourselves to citing a single recent work with a lengthy bibliography for each point.

For Section 3, we interviewed ten native signers of ASL: four in Austin, Texas, one in Washington, DC, and five in the Philadelphia area. All grew up in those areas; all identify as white. The term "native signers" as used in Sections 3 and 4 indicates people born to deaf signing parents who use sign language as their mother language, regardless of whether or not they are themselves deaf. All our consultants are deaf except one. Two were older (58 and 61), and the rest were between 19 and mid 30s.

We noted few differences in the signing of our consultants with respect to taboo and none related to geography. We vetted our findings with several deaf people who have been signing most of their lives and with additional native deaf signers, from varying geographic regions, and received confirmation. One of the anonymous referees of the published article that Section 4 is based on self-identified as a native signer and made several confirmatory comments and none nonconfirmatory.

In light of our remarks in Section 1.4, in particular, it may seem ironic that our consultants were native signers and white. Further, for this study we didn't even note gender. There are two reasons for this. One is simply that the data were gathered in 2011, when the focus in research was strongly on native signers, and when attention to demographic factors was not so strong as today. But the other is that, because of the sensitivity of the material, we gathered data from groups of family and friends, where a member of the group would invite people to their house to meet with us, giving the kind of informal social atmosphere that eased what might have otherwise been guarded conversation. It simply turned out, then, that the groups were native signers and white, though gender identity varied. We now describe our data-gathering method and urge others to try it with groups that have different demographics from the ones we studied.

Study of casual spoken language today is arguably best done using large databases of spontaneous conversation properly annotated (e.g., the Linguistic Data Consortium of the University of Pennsylvania, www.ldc.upenn.edu). Such databases are few for sign. An overview of datasets for the sign languages of Europe (Project-Easier 2021) and a large data set for Auslan (www.auslan.org. au/) are available, as are smaller data sets for other sign languages. For ASL, two large data bases are ASL-LEX (Caselli et al. 2017) and SignBank (Neidle et al. 2022), which were not available when we gathered data (in 2011). While writing the present work, we searched these data bases for the taboo items discussed here. Many were missing, which is no surprise: the very nature of taboo might be responsible for this lack, since consultants might not always be forthcoming or willing to be recorded using taboo items. Those items that do appear did not add new information to our discussion and we note that some were, according to our consultants, older forms of the signs (e.g., LESBIAN). (Throughout signs are written in small capitals; see Baker-Shenk and Cokely 1991). Perhaps the nature of being recorded for such a site makes one think of posterity and affects one's choice of pronunciation. Our perusal of a few data bases leads us to suspect that our method of data gathering – using close to a conversational context, with friends and relatives (see Llisterri 1992) – might still be among the most fruitful ways to study taboo. By putting together people who know each other and (some of) us well, we hoped our consultants would be forthcoming. This turned out to be the case; we sensed no inhibitions.

Two of the authors are native signers, one deaf, one hearing; one grew up in the Austin area, one in the Philadelphia area; both were under forty at the time of collecting the data. These facts may have been conducive in our process. Our work with consultants took place in casual settings: two older consultants hosted gatherings of friends in their home, and wound up being drawn into the conversation. While these two consultants use the terms discussed here, they report using them infrequently. Despite this, their contributions were copious. We asked all participants to demonstrate how they use in conversation the terms they identify as taboo. Sometimes we jumped in to ask if certain sentences were possible. For example, if someone negated an utterance with NONE, we would ask if one could negate it with NEVER. Quick, direct, and simple questions usually led to thorough discussions with subtle insights into differences between relatively similar utterances. Often when one person brought up a term, another expanded on its use and the conversation would take off, as though we researchers were no longer there, with joking and spontaneous language that supplied additional examples. This was particularly true of the bleached taboo predicates discussed in Section 4. When we were familiar with a bleached taboo term from our own experience and it didn't come up in the first hour of conversation, we explicitly asked if our consultants had ever seen or used it. Every time the answer was positive and the conversation again became lively and fecund.

When analyzing the data gathered in this way, we sometimes needed to return to our consultants to seek examples crucial to deciding between analyses. For this, we approached our original consultants individually, for their convenience and to see if more variation on acceptability judgments arose when they were not together. We asked general questions that might reveal syntactic structure. For example, pronoun copies of the subject tagged onto the end of a sentence (such as YOUR SISTER GO HOME, SHE?; see Padden 1988) generally refer to the matrix subject only. So we would ask whether subject tags could be added to a complex sentence that had come up in one of the hosted gatherings and which tags, specifically, or whether they could come up with a scenario in which one started a conversation with a particular utterance from a hosted gathering. In this way, we elicited sentences they considered grammatical and ones they considered ungrammatical. We found no variation in their judgments with respect to the types of sentences elicited. The two of us who are native signers agree with all the grammaticality judgments presented in this paper.

For Section 4, data judgments were again collected through a qualitative study in casual situations in the Philadelphia and Washington, DC deaf communities. Nine deaf, sighted, white consultants participated, four men (two gay, two straight) and five women (three gay, two straight), between the ages of twenty-five and fifty. Additionally, a CODA relative of one of the authors was included – male, straight, thirty years old. His judgments coincided with those of at least two deaf participants. Two of the authors of this paper felt comfortable participating actively in the discussions for this section since they are members of those deaf communities (one in each). Their judgments likewise always coincided with those of at least two deaf participants.

The technique of using informal gatherings to collect data is known as Think Aloud Protocol (TAP; van Someren, Barnard & Sandberg 1994). TAP has been adapted in sign language studies with respect to choices sign language interpreters make (Stone 2009) and choices mimes and sign language poets make in performances (Sutton-Spence & Boyes Braem 2013). In linguistics in general, TAP has been used fruitfully in studying how people look at their own language habits regarding translation and shifting between an L1 and an L2 (Cifuentes-Férez & Rojo 2015; Künzli 2009). Certainly, one can challenge the extent to which TAP can give information about spontaneous language use. We repeat only that we sensed no inhibitions among our consultants and that the discussions rang true to those of us who are members of the deaf communities studied here.

3 Taboo across the Grammar of ASL

Taboo expressions creatively exploit the grammar in many languages. For example, diminutives often carry an evaluative component that may be pejorative (comparable in English to something like 'puny little fellow'), as happens in Italian and German (Dressler & Barbaresi 2011) and colloquial Jordanian Arabic (Badarneh 2010). The same is true of elative compounds in Dutch, in which the first element of the compound serves as a modifier denoting a high degree of the property associated with the second (head) element (comparable in English to something like "dirt poor"; Hoeksema 2012). Here we look at such creativity in ASL regarding the lexicon, the syntax, and nonmanuals.

3.1 Taboo Terms and the Lexicon

At the level of individual signs, taboo terms play with phonological parameters. Here we exemplify five types of such play, often, but not strictly, humorous. Undoubtedly, more variants of the taboo terms discussed here exist, but our goal is to be representative, rather than exhaustive. While the taboo terms here are phonologically or morphologically creative in a number of ways, all those ways are also employed in creative language that does not involve taboo terms (such as jokes) and sometimes even in the ordinary lexicon. Thus, studying the coining of taboo terms reinforces what we know about creativity in ASL in general.

3.1.1 Manual Letter Handshapes

ASL has a manual alphabet with handshapes standing for letters, and manual numerals with handshapes standing for numbers. (The appendix gives the handshapes referred to.) Manual alphabets are used in fingerspelling text of the

Figure 1 One variant of HELL

Figure 2 B-S

ambient spoken language. Different sign languages can have different manual alphabets and incorporate use of the manual alphabet to different extents and in different ways in everyday conversation (Quinto-Pozos & Adam 2015: 36–42).

Using the manual letter handshape of the first letter of the corresponding English word in making a sign is called initialization (as in FAMILY, KITCHEN, NURSE), and it is common in ASL. A more complex form of initialization can occur when an ASL sign corresponds to an English compound (whether or not the ASL sign is a compound). Sometimes the handshape starts out as the first letter of the first element of the English compound and then changes to the first letter of the second element of the English compound (as in WORKSHOP: W>S). Less commonly, one can find initialization coupled with what one might call "finalization": the handshape begins as the first letter of the corresponding English word and then changes to the final letter of that word (LINGUISTICS: L>S).

Some taboo terms employ initialization. Figure 1 shows a variant of HELL with the H-handshape.[1] Figure 2 shows one of the signs for "bullshit" built on the corresponding English compound. It starts with B that changes to S. We gloss

---

[1] The figures in Sections 3 and 4 are elicited examples.

this particular sign B-S. In older varieties of ASL another variant glossed BULLSHIT has the same handshape change, but is located in front of the mouth. In both, the manual letters correspond to the first letters of the elements of the English compound. We will see examples of initialization plus "finalization" in later subsections.

3.1.2 Exploitation of Connotations Associated with Phonological Parameters

In spoken languages, many take the position that the relationship between articulation and meaning is arbitrary; this is a basic principle in the comparative method of historical linguistics (e.g., Winter 1970). Nevertheless, phonesthemes (submorphemic sound clusters that can appear in words with similar meanings, such as the initial [st] in English in *stupid, stop, stump, stultify*, etc.) have long been acknowledged in many spoken languages (e.g., Abelin 1999 for Swedish; Zorc 1990 for Astronesian). In sign languages, nonarbitrary relationships between articulation and meaning are commonplace, including the equivalent of phonesthemes: one can create signs by exploiting connotations associated with phonological parameters, some of which may be iconic and perhaps even morphological (Johnston & Ferrara 2012). Here we take a peek at some of these connotations exploited in taboo language.

Various locations have connotations strong enough to allow a family of signs to form around them. Signs made at the side of the forehead often have to do with cognition (KNOW, THINK, REASON, IMAGINE, DREAM, etc.). Creative language, particularly in jokes, exploits such connotations (e.g., Klima & Bellugi 1975). Exploiting location connotations is a common way to coin taboo terms. One insult of taboo-strength related to the ASL cognition family just mentioned is to take the sign HEARING and change its location from in front of the lips to in front of the forehead, to mean THINK-LIKE-A-HEARING-PERSON (Figure 3). This sign is

Figure 3 HEARING and THINK-LIKE-A-HEARING-PERSON

derogatory because it indicates a person who displays behaviors typical of hearing people, going contrary to deaf tendencies (Wilcox 2000: 93–94).

The nose is the location of a handful of signs denoting unpleasant things (UGLY, BORING, SNOB, etc.) and, while many signs without a pejorative connotation are made at the nose (MOUSE, FUNNY, SILLY, etc.), that location used to be reserved for slang or taboo signs (Schein & Stewart 1995), and is still employed in coining insults. In the 1980s there was a television soap opera called *Dynasty*. Deaf people in the Philadelphia area who didn't like the program used the name sign of a D at the forehead, then N at the nose, then Y at the chin – with the palm oriented toward the signer. They were building on the fact that the letters D, N, Y occur in that order in the name of the program. But each letter also carried meaning because of its location. D at the forehead evoked the idea of dumb (DUMB, STUPID, NO-BRAINS are all made there). Y at the chin is the sign WRONG. But what is most relevant to our point is that N at the nose contributed a pejorative sense because of unpleasant connotations of that location (and compare to the English phonestheme [sn] in *snot, snobby, snooty, snivel*, etc.). While this name sign is an insult, it does not use a taboo term, nor does it have the force of a taboo. We mention it to show that in coining new signs the nose can lend a pejorative connotation.

There are various taboo signs that mean "shit." One is made with the radial side of the S handshape near the nose followed by either a wrist nod (Figure 4) or a shoulder rotation lowering the forearm so that the hand moves away from the nose. We contend that the location allows the sign to exploit the pejorative connotations associated with the nose, particularly needed since this sign isn't iconic (cf. the highly iconic variant described just before Figure 7).

3.1.3 Compounding and Incorporation

Compounding occurs frequently in ASL (PAJAMAS < SLEEP^CLOTHES, SOFT-HEARTED < SOFT^HEART, PARENTS < MOTHER^FATHER; where "^" indicates compound juncture). One input sign temporally follows the other, often with

Figure 4 Variant of SHIT made at the nose

Figure 5 PISS-OFF

spreading phonological features (handshape and orientation) and reduction of movement (repetition is eliminated), so that sometimes the input signs for lexicalized compounds are difficult to recognize (Liddell & Johnson 1986). Compounding can occur between a taboo and a non-taboo sign to create a new taboo sign. FUCK-UP is made with FUCK (two Vs tapping each other, palms facing) followed by UP (the thumbs-up version of UP).

It's not always obvious if a sign is a compound. In PISS-OFF (Figure 5), P>F (the first and last letters of *piss off*), we have initialization and "finalization." However, this is not the full story. PEE is a tap of P on the nose tip. PISS-OFF starts as PEE, then the wrist twists away and the handshape changes to F. We suggest that compounding has applied: PEE^OFF. While the sign clearly starts as PEE, it is not obvious that it ends as OFF. OFF is made with B moving off the nondominant hand into neutral space (in front of the upper torso), palm orientation changing from down to up. However, given that the starting point for the second element of this compound is the nose, if that element were, in fact, OFF, the twist away from the nose as the hand moves into neutral space (resulting in palm orientation change) is expected. So, we have initialization coupled with "finalization" in a compound rather than a simple sign.

Another word-coining process in which a whole sign can appear within another is incorporation, a variety of word-formation processes where one word is fused inside another. Incorporation is common in ASL, typically of numerals appearing as the handshape in another time sign (DAY, MONTH, etc.; see Liddell and Johnson 1989). Additionally, Supalla (1992) analyzes many name signs as involving incorporation.

Often it is difficult to distinguish between compounding and incorporation. A taboo sign, for example, can appear inside another sign as an insult. For example, Alexander Graham Bell was a leading exponent of oralism in the late 1800s; accordingly, his name sign is a play on his initials (Mirus 2008), seen in

Figure 6 Insulting play on initials of Alexander Graham Bell

Figure 6. It consists of A, G, and B at the forehead. A on the forehead is DUMB; G, PEA-BRAIN; and B, BASTARD.

3.1.4 Blending

Blending is a word-formation process whereby phonological properties of one lexical item are combined with those of another to make a new lexical item whose meaning reflects a combination of the meanings of the input (*smog* < *smoke+fog*). Blending is distinct from coining via exploitation of connotations associated with phonological parameters. With the latter we use a general association of some (underdetermined) sense with a phonological parameter in coining a new sign. But in blending, we merge phonological properties of two signs, where perhaps each of the input signs could be iconic, but neither is built on a phonological parameter that has a strong connotation.

Blending is seen in STRICT. HARD is two-handed: bent V-handshapes are arranged one above the other, each with the palm oriented contralaterally; the ulnar side of the higher hand and the radial side of the lower hand hit together. NOSE is made by touching the nose with the 1-handshape. STRICT is made by touching the nose with the side of the bent-V – which we suggest is literally HARD-NOSE – blending the handshape and palm orientation of HARD with the location and movement of NOSE. (This is not a calque: a calque would be a compound in ASL.)

One can blend an ordinary and a taboo sign to make a new taboo sign. When deaf schools compete in sports, sometimes they make up taboo name signs for the other school (Rutherford 1993). Sophara Sok and Rebecca Furland (personal communication, spring 2011) offer an example regarding the deaf school from Louisiana. Its ordinary sign name is L-A, with the hand moving ipsilaterally. SHIT is made with the nondominant A and the dominant A, which has the thumb extended so that it is inserted within the nondominant A. The thumb moves out, going at a diagonal downward and ipsilaterally (iconic of defecation). The insult name sign for the Louisiana Deaf school uses a nondominant A and a dominant L, where the thumb of the L starts out inside the nondominant

Figure 7 (Insulting) name sign for Louisiana

Figure 8 MOTHER and MOTHERFUCKER

A and moves out, downward and ipsilaterally, and changes to an A (Figure 7): the L-A name sign has been blended with SHIT to form the taboo name sign. Interestingly, some younger deaf people use this sign in a nonpejorative way to indicate the state, not limiting it to the school.

Blending also occurs between a sign and a taboo gesture. UNDERSTAND is produced by the side of the forehead and made with S>1, palm oriented to the rear. If 1 is replaced with the extended middle-finger gesture meaning "fuck you" (hereafter "the taboo finger gesture"), the result means "I get it and you can fuck off." This is blending rather than incorporation, since the taboo gesture alone does not call for a handshape change, but the sign UNDERSTAND does. So phonological input from both signs is blended.

Another sign-gesture blend involves MOTHER, a one-handed sign made with 5 tapping the chin. If the handshape is replaced with the taboo finger gesture, the thumb extended, we get the blend MOTHERFUCKER (Figure 8).

Another blend for MOTHERFUCKER has 3 with a bent wrist tap on the chin, then move ipsilaterally and then down, following the 7-path shape, to neutral space. The chin is the location of MOTHER. The ending location is that of FUCK (the two-handed

Figure 9 Insulting name sign PHILADELPHIA

variant in which the hands meet, palms facing). The 3 and the bent wrist, however, are not found in either MOTHER (which uses 5) or FUCK (which uses V), so this is more complex than a simple blend. By opening the thumb (as V>3), contact at the chin can be the same as in MOTHER. This sign was observed in Austin, Texas, where it was used with distinctly sassy dynamics. The 3-handshape and the bent wrist might be independent features taken from rapping, where they are common.

Another plausible example of blending relies even more heavily on iconicity. PHILADELPHIA is P tracing the 7-path in neutral space. An insult name sign for Philadelphia is two handed; the dominant hand forms a P and the nondominant forms an S. The middle finger of the P comes down from above and dips inside the S twice, iconic of anal intercourse (Figure 9). The actual sign ANAL-INTERCOURSE has a nondominant 1 poking through the circle of a dominant F. This insult name sign does not at first look like a blend of PHILADELPHIA and ANAL-INTERCOURSE for two reasons. First, the dominant is doing the poking action. Second, the hand poked into is not an F, but an S. Both differences, however, follow from phonological restrictions. In a two-handed asymmetrical sign, typically one hand moves while the other serves as a base (or location) for movement. Usually the base handshape is unmarked: 1, 5, A, B, C, O, S (Battison 1978). If the P of PHILADELPHIA (which is per force the dominant hand since this is a one-handed sign) is to be maintained in the blended insult, then the dominant hand must be a P. That entails that the dominant hand will be the one doing the dipping (since there's nowhere for anything to dip into that P). Now consider the nondominant hand. We'd expect it to be the F seen in ANAL-INTERCOURSE. But F is not an unmarked handshape. The only unmarked hand-shapes that offer the opportunity for being dipped into are S and O. S was chosen, perhaps to evoke the nondominant A in SHIT (where A is just S with the thumb beside the curled fingers), and perhaps because F has different selected fingers from P (Mandel 1981). Thus, this insult name sign is a blend of PHILADELPHIA and ANAL-INTERCOURSE.

a. Dominant hand is V   b. Dominant hand is P

Figure 10 One variant of FUCK-UP

Figure 11 Another variant of FUCK-UP

3.1.5 Combinations

The various methods of coining signs can combine. We already saw initialization combining with other word-formation processes. Now we will look at additional types of combinations.

In Section 3.1.3, we mentioned a compound variation of FUCK-UP (FUCK^UP). Other variations are more complex. In the variant in Figure 10, the hands sign FUCK (Vs tap each other, but now only once in Figure 10a), then the dominant hand changes to P as the hands tap against each other a second time (in Figure 10b). The second part is a blend of FUCK with fingerspelled U-P (hyphens between letters indicate fingerspelling). Note that U-P has lost the initial U. Since U and V are variants of one another (closed versus spread), maybe V replaced the U of U-P, so that the nondominant hand gives us V, approximating the U of U-P, while the dominant hand gives us P.

In another variant of FUCK-UP the nondominant hand is 5 in neutral space, palm up, while the dominant is 3, above it, but not touching. The dominant hand contacts the nondominant hand, as 3>10 (Figure 11).

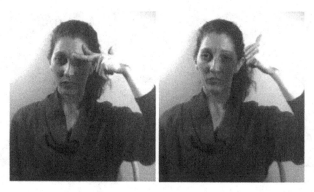

Figure 12 One variant of FUCK-UP-IN-THE-HEAD

Here the V of FUCK is replaced by the unmarked 5 on the nondominant hand and an initial 3 on the dominant. Since 3 shows up in the Austin, Texas variant for MOTHERFUCKER, we might propose that 3 is independently associated with obscenities. Alternatively (and preferably), there is a phonological account. The phonological difference between V and 3 is closed verses open thumb. The opening of a closed thumb is also seen in the lexicalized fingerspelling loan sign #NO. The tucked-in thumb of N, when paired with the following O, is replaced by the open thumb, which meets the extended fingertips to form O. Perhaps the same kind of phenomenon is at play here: in anticipation of the thumb opening and the other fingers closing into 10, the thumb opens (V>3) so it is in the correct position for 10.

Finally, there are various signs we gloss FUCK-UP-IN-THE-HEAD. One variant is one-handed made at the forehead (Figure 12). 3 (with index finger touching or near forehead) changes to 10 as it moves forward. Another variant is identical, except the middle finger of 3 starts out in contact with the forehead. A third variant starts with both fingers of 3 in contract with the forehead, then 3>10 moving ipsilaterally. All these variants describe someone who is drunk or on drugs; they exploit the cognitive-connotation association with the location of forehead as they blend and compound, using that (complicit) 3 again.

3.1.6 Implications

Humor is a key factor in whether a slang term is memorable, and memorability affects whether a slang term is evanescent or remains in the language for years (Labov 1992: section 6). Since taboo terms are used in many of the same social conditions in which slang is used (Andersson & Trudgill 1990), we might expect humor to be a factor in whether a taboo term disappears quickly or gets entrenched. The taboo terms discussed thus far are humorous (though they can be true insults) and well-entrenched, adding evidence that humor is relevant to memorability of new lexical items. The entrenchment of taboo terms might be of particularly strong importance in deaf communities since the use of humor in creating a close linguistic community and in establishing one's membership in it is strong among deaf communities, at least in the USA and the UK (Sutton-Spence & Napoli 2009).

3.2 Taboo Expressions and the Syntax

Taboo expressions can appear isolated, embedded within larger syntactic structures, or as whole sentences that serve to emphasize or to give new information about the previous sentence.

3.2.1 Syntactically Isolated Taboo Terms

Taboo in ASL can function in many of the same ways as in spoken language with a similar range of lexical items and rude tone. Among exclamations we find HELL, DAMN, and SHIT. A common malediction is FUCK-YOU: the taboo finger gesture moves upward, middle finger up. (Arguably, this is not a sign, but the gesture found in spoken language, as well.[2]) Another frequently used taboo is the loan sign F-K! (the lexicalized fingerspelling), which can be a malediction (as in F-K, directed toward a spatial index, to mean *Fuck that!*). Name calling is also common, such as variants of ASSHOLE (A-H and an F-handshape), SLUT and PUSSY. Often anatomical and taboo terms are distinguishable only by movement dynamics and nonmanuals. VAGINA, the anatomical term, differs from PUSSY, the name-calling taboo term, in that the latter calls for quick, sharp movement and sometimes an angry (or perhaps joking) facial expression.

3.2.2 Syntactically Embedded Taboo Terms

Taboo terms can serve other conversational functions. They can be referential noun phrases (NPs; *I hate that bitch*) or predicates (*He's a real ass-wipe/He fucks up everything.*). Such uses occur in ASL, not surprisingly, given that taboo items occur in name-calling and maledictions. In spoken language we also find taboo pejorative modifiers (*the professor from hell*), degree adverbials (*scared shitless*), and emphasizers in a wide variety of syntactic structures (*What the fuck is she talking about? Get the hell out of here! Like fuck I will!*). Other languages of Europe also exhibit wide ranges of taboo uses, which can tell us about the syntactic structure of the language at a given time since the taboo terms are embedded within

---

[2] Gestures with precise meanings that can be used in the absence of speech are called emblems, and can serve as the source of linguistic elements in sign languages (Wilcox 2009).

larger structures (Hoeksema & Napoli 2019). These uses can often be purely emphatic (although vulgarity is still present; hence, they are taboo).

Comparable emphatic uses of taboo terms embedded in larger syntactic structures in ASL are hard to find. We have not yet found taboo terms that serve as pejorative modifiers (nothing like *She's a fucking bully*), nor taboo terms that serve as degree adverbials (nothing like *She's so fucking beautiful*). However, we have found taboo terms used for emphasis in other syntactic structures. It will turn out useful to organize our discussion in comparison with English examples. ASL and English are not genetically related, of course, but ASL signers come into contact with English often.

In (1) the taboo term is emphatic:

(1)   Get the fuck out of bed.

We could convey the same command without the taboo term:

(2)   Get out of bed.

but the addition of the taboo term adds urgency. In other sentences, the taboo term is crucial for grammaticality:

(3)   She beat the hell out of him.

(4)   *She beat out of him.

While the taboo term in (3) fills the grammatical function of direct object, its conversational function is to carry emphasis. ASL also uses taboo terms for emphasis, but not generally with intransitive verbs. The only exception we have found is a taboo term used with the intransitive verb we'll gloss FINISH, which consists of a 5-handshape extended forward and trilled (shaking rapidly), palm facing contralaterally. The taboo term F-K, seen in (5), or the taboo finger gesture can emphasize this sign, shown in Figure 13.

Figure 13 F-K FINISH

(5)   F-K FINISH!
        "That's fucking enough already."

There is a FINISH aspectual marker and a FINISH verb. FINISH in (5) is the verb, an order to stop doing something; (5) does not mean that a sexual act should end, which is the reading we would get if F-K was verb and FINISH was aspectual marker.

The nonmanuals give evidence that (5) is a single clause (Nicodemus 2009): we observed no lengthening of signs, eye blink, body leans, hand clasping, cheek puffing, nose wrinkling, or changes in head position or eye aperture between F-K and FINISH.

In English taboo NPs used for emphasis eschew sentence-final position,

(6)   Shut the fuck up!

(7)   *Shut up the fuck!

although they may be sentence-final in elliptical expressions (*What the fuck?*). This might be due to the history of this emphatic use of taboo expressions; they might have arisen via analogy with taboo expressions that originally were true direct objects followed by prepositional phrases (PPs; *Beat the {devil/shit/fuck} out of him*). Since direct objects come between the verb and a following PP, that would be the natural position for the emphatic taboo expression.

Interestingly, ASL also disfavors sentence-final position for emphatic taboo NPs. Our consultants felt uncomfortable moving F-K to follow FINISH in (5). (5) has no direct object, but discomfort with a sentence-final emphatic taboo term holds even when a direct object is present: our consultants did not like (8) when HELL (as in Figure 1) was moved to sentence-final position.

(8)   GIRL SCARE HELL ME.
        "The girl scared the hell out of me."
        (cf. *GIRL SCARE ME HELL.)

English can also insert a taboo NP after a wh-word for emphasis (*How in fuck's name can I respond to that?*). This also occurs in ASL with the lexicalized fingerspelled F-U-C-K:

(9)   WHERE F-U-C-K HE GO?
        "Where the fuck did he go?"

(10)   WHAT HELL YOU {BEHAVE/ACT}?
        "What the hell are you doing?"

Our consultants between the ages of twenty-two and thirty-two told us they could use the taboo finger gesture instead of F-U-C-K in (9), where the youngest claimed this was commonly seen among students at Gallaudet, where he was a student. Our older consultants did not accept the taboo finger gesture here. (The variant of "what" used in (10) was a dominant 1 hitting and moving down and across a nondominant B.)

While (5) was produced spontaneously, (8–10) were produced only after we questioned our consultants specifically about such constructions. We suspect (8–10), and maybe even (5), is due to contact with English. Why? First, discomfort with the emphatic taboo appearing in sentence-final position in (5) and (8) looks like English influence (recall that our consultants are well educated). Second, the possibility of the taboo finger gesture in (9) seems like influence from its use among hearing people. Third, the use of an independent lexical item to emphasize another lexical item is not characteristic of ASL. Scholars of sign literature (Robinson 2006) and teachers of ASL (Grayson 2003) agree that intensification in ASL is handled by nonmanuals or modulating movement (Bridges & Metzger 1996). Linguists seeking a unified syntactic account of the lack of manual degree modifiers and of taboo-terms used as intensifiers might propose that these items fill a single syntactic slot and that ASL lacks this slot (though other sign languages may not). We take a different approach here, appealing to timing considerations. But whatever the explanation, the use of taboo items to emphasize other signs would be atypical of ASL, casting doubt on the naturalness of (5) and (8–10). Finally, WHERE in ASL is more likely to occur in sentence-final position than sentence-initial position, but in (9–10), word order corresponds closely to English.

3.2.3 Resultative Taboo Classifier Sentences Used as Emphasizers

In English, one can make emphatic a sentence like *She's beautiful* by adding a taboo term, including a resultative indicating degree: *She's {fucking/drop-dead} beautiful* (Hoeksema & Napoli 2019). In ASL, our consultants do not do this. Instead, they emphasize such a sentence by following it with a separate sentence about an explicitly sexual result:

(11)   SHE BEAUTIFUL. GET-ERECTION.

This means something like "She's so beautiful, it makes me hard." The second sentence is a classifier construction: a 1-handshape classifier near the waist shoots from pointing down to forward.

Sometimes these explicitly sexual resultative sentences do not emphasize a previous assertion, but give new information about the situation. The classifier sentence in (11) (the second sentence) might then follow a sentence like LOOK-AT-HER, without any mention of her attractiveness. Likewise, one might sign:

(12)   OPEN-DOOR. NIPPLES-STIFFEN.

(13)   OPEN-DOOR. BALLS-SHRINK.

These mean something like "I opened the door. It was so cold my {nipples got hard/balls shrank}." (In context, the subject need not be first person.) For (12–13), again, the taboo sentences consist of classifiers. These taboo classifier sentences have a humorous flair (cf., *It was cold enough to freeze the balls off a brass monkey.*)

3.3 Nonlexical Ways of Conveying Taboo-Level Rudeness, Insults, or Emphasis: Phonetic Properties and the Nonmanuals

While ASL does not typically insert taboo terms for emphasis, it doubles (Petronio 1993) or copies (Lillo-Martin 1991) signs, or increases the movement speed (Coulter 1990) or size of signs. Even more commonly, emphasis is expressed through appropriate nonmanuals, which can amount to taboo.

3.3.1 Nonmanuals

Nonmanuals can convey lexical, grammatical, and affective information (Pfau & Quer 2010; Herrmann & Steinbach 2013; Lackner 2017; Pendzich 2020). They can be superimposed across a string of manual signs, and they can occur without the manuals. Nonmanuals can convey rudeness in sign languages all on their own (Hoza 2008); conversely, they are keys to mitigating potentially rude comments. While studies that look at affective nonmanuals regarding politeness in sign languages deal mainly with register (Hoza 2007), George (2011), who examines Japanese Sign Language, proposes that affective nonmanuals have typological salience across sign languages as the crucial factor in politeness versus rudeness.

Nonmanuals conveying politeness are easily distinguished from other nonmanuals. In a study of requests in ASL, Roush (2007), building on Hoza (2007), found five nonmanuals with functions specific to sign as opposed to spoken language. A polite pucker (puckering and protruding the lips) indicates solidarity and is a signal of a cooperative stance. Tight lips can be used to mitigate moderate impositions. A polite grimace (with clinched teeth) mitigates more serious threats to face, and a polite grimace frown mitigates severe threats to face. Finally, the body-head teeter (rocking body and head from side to side) can mitigate extreme impositions associated with difficult requests or rejections.

Nonmanuals conveying rudeness are often complex or context-dependent. For example, nose wrinkling can insult (Wilbur 1987), but it can also be lexically required. Widening eyes can insult (Wilbur 2011), but narrowing eyes can add emphasis, which in context can be rude. A stiff upright torso can indicate a superior attitude, while a torso leaning forward can be aggressive or, simply, interested. A tight face, with lips pursed, cheeks bunched, and eyebrows lowered, typically goes with an angry outburst. A deadpan face can show sarcasm. A protruding tongue can be obscene. Gazing away can be rude, signaling that one has exited the conversation (Lewis & Henderson 1997). When used in conjunction with taboo signs, many nonmanuals enhance the taboo (Loos, Cramer & Napoli 2020).

3.3.2 Mimicry and Manual Codes

Playing with phonetic properties and nonmanuals is typical of constructed dialogue in ASL. One kind of insulting constructed dialogue is mimicking someone's language. In spoken language, mimicry is used to great effect when a speaker ridicules a nonnative speaker. In a sign language, pointing out differences in language can be jest, or a biting insult, strong enough to be considered taboo. Mimicry can involve the lexicon, the morphology, and the syntax, but always involves phonetic properties and nonmanuals.

One way to insult people learning a sign language (whether they are hearing, deaf who are new to sign, or signers of another sign language) is to mimic with large, jerky movements and cramped or wild handshapes, yielding gobbledy-gook. Such insults can be made ruder by including whole body movements (twirling, leaping) or impermissible locations for signs (middle of the back, bottom of the foot). In all this, nonmanuals show the idiocy of the person mimicked (vacant gaze, sideways protruding tongue).

It is not uncommon to insult spoken language in general and, hence, hearing people in general. One insult is to mimic a hearing person's speech by moving the lips quickly, keeping the face deadpan. Movement of the lips alone might appear to be merely a weird muscular behavior – but the nonmanuals tell us this is mimicry of speech, since hearing people are notorious for lacking facial expression as they chatter.

Another insult with respect to how hearing people sign is to use one of the forms of Manually Coded English (MCE) when mimicking. Signers thus demonstrate that they know what MCE is and that it is not ASL. This second point is important, since many hearing people either have no idea that ASL is not a manual version of English or have tried to push MCE on deaf people, often with the misguided assumption that this would aid in gaining literacy. This kind of mockery can be at once a rebellion against an ineffective educational policy and a show of pride in the communicative superiority of ASL over MCE. The face is where we learn whether this is light jest, lethal insult, or something between.

3.4 Concluding Remarks

Sign languages and spoken languages employ a range of taboo terms in exclamations, name calling, and maledictions. They use taboo terms as referential NPs and as predicates. They can have whole taboo resultative clauses that give emphasis to some other clause. And they exploit phonetic properties to support the intent in these taboo expressions. Further, they can employ a single mechanism to convey rudeness as well as emphasis. In sign, that single mechanism is the nonmanuals. In spoken language that single mechanism is taboo terms.

4 Bleached Taboo-Term Predicates in ASL

Study of bleached predicates reveals information about the grammar of ASL that, to our knowledge, has not been discussed elsewhere and is not revealed by study of other types of predicates. The taboo terms here involve religion and sex and, with one exception, they are historically based on taboo-terms that have lost their charge (hence, are bleached); many signers use them today without intending rudeness or vulgarity, nor with negative connotation. While some deaf people might consider these examples inappropriate for polite conversation, others, especially younger signers, do not, although a few have told us they still retain enough sensitivity to the historical roots that they would not use them in a classroom or synagogue. This kind of semantic bleaching is noted for taboo items in various languages (*shit* in *I've got a lot of shit to take care of this weekend*, and *suck* in *Having to redo this paper really sucks*). Our glosses of these predicates indicate their historical sense (reflected in their phonological shape), so these glosses are vulgar, while the translations in English indicate their bleached sense in ASL today, showing they are not vulgar.

In Section 2, we discussed data collection for this section. In addition, however, we videotaped one signer, who made up utterances using bleached taboo predicates without knowing the particular linguistic issues we were concerned with at the time. These tapes form the basis for our discussion of intonational phrase markers in Section 4.2. While head-on videotapes of a single signer allow one to see the full range of potential markers of intonational phrase boundaries (difficult to capture in videos of spontaneous conversation), videotapes of a mock situation limit what one can glean regarding natural intonation. Our purpose in making these videotapes was to help clarify

Figure 14 BULLSHIT

the intuitions of the two native signers among our authors. Sometimes the videotaped signer produced several variations on a given utterance, sometimes only one. All taped utterances were judged grammatical by our consultants. Each of the three coauthors watched the video clips independently at regular speed and noted intonational cues. We then watched the clips in slow motion for a self-check. Our findings were cross-checked among us.

4.1 Conversion between Ordinary Noun and Predicate

Many signs are glossed as BULLSHIT in ASL. One uses the horn handshape (1-I in Figure 14) moving forward in neutral space with palm facing the signer. It is often used in crude interjections, but can appear without pejorative sense. For example, if someone said something funny and you knew it couldn't be true, you might laugh and make this sign.

Another one-handed sign meaning "bullshit" is B-S (in Figure 2). For some of our consultants (all young, but not regionally identifiable), the movement of the sign is toward the addressee or an appropriate spatial index (that is, a point in space that has been designated to represent a referent, by pointing to it with finger, chin, lip, head tilt, or gaze; see Neidle and colleagues 2000), where the addressee or the referent of the spatial index is understood to be the recipient. Across sign languages, this kind of directionality of movement is a characteristic of action signs only (as opposed to state or process signs; Schwager & Zeshan 2008). For these signers, we analyze B-S as an agreeing verb (a verb whose movement parameter is a line from the spatial index of one of the verb's arguments to the spatial index of another; see Pfau, Salzmann and Steinbach 2018) with the motion being toward the verb's recipient argument. In contrast, we call the B-S that is made in neutral space "non-directional" so as to avoid any label prejudicial to its analysis. In our discussion, we look at nondirectional B-S only, and return briefly to agreeing verb B-S at the end of this section.

What word class do BULLSHIT in Figure 14 and nondirectional B-S in Figure 1 belong to? Evidence shows they are nouns. First, consider the independent sign ZERO/ NONE as a negative (as contrasted to the clitic –ZERO; see Aronoff and colleagues 2004). ZERO/ NONE negates nouns but not verbs, and follows them (Wood 1999). BULLSHIT and nondirectional B-S can be negated with a following NONE, indicating they are nouns:

(14)   BULLSHIT NONE.
        "This is not bullshit/ This is the truth."

(15)   B-S NONE.
        "This is not bullshit/ This is the truth."

Second, BULLSHIT collocates as a noun. ACCEPT is subcategorized to take as direct object an NP or a clause. But if the direct object is a clause, that clause will have a subject. In other words, we don't have bare verbs as the complement of ACCEPT (in contrast to verbs like TRY).

(16)   YOU NOT ACCEPT GIFT.
        "You don't accept the gift."
        YOU NOT ACCEPT {HE/YOU/I} COMICS READ.
        "You don't accept the fact that {he/you/I} read comics."
        *YOU NOT ACCEPT COMICS READ.
        "You don't accept reading comics."

BULLSHIT can occur as the direct object of ACCEPT, as in (17).

(17)   (A.) YOU ACCEPT BULLSHIT (FROM HIM).
        "You accept bullshit (from him)."
        (B.) I ACCEPT BULLSHIT? YOU CRAZY. I ACCEPT FLOWERS, CANDY, PERFUME.
        "I accept bullshit? You're crazy. I accept flowers, candy, perfume."

Again, those signers who accept (15) also allow nondirectional B-S in (17) in place of BULLSHIT. These data follow if BULLSHIT and nondirectional B-S are nouns.

Other evidence shows they are verbs. Nouns cannot take aspectual inflection in sign languages (Voghel 2005), although some can be inflected for number (Pizzuto & Corazza 1996; Pfau & Steinbach 2006). In contrast, verbs exhibit a range of aspectual inflection (Wilbur 2005). If a one-handed verb such as EAT has continuative aspect, often both hands make alternating circles. Additionally, adjectives can exhibit continuative inflection to yield new adjectives with the sense of characteristic behavior (such as TACITURN<QUIET; see Padden & Perlmutter 1987). Nouns, however, do not take continuative aspect. Thus, BOOK cannot take continuative aspect (despite how many one reads); instead,

Figure 15 BULLSHITTING (BULLSHIT with continuative aspect)

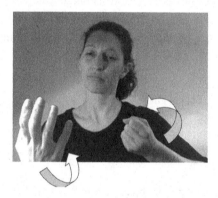

Figure 16 B-S-ING (B-S with continuative aspect; handshape change
and movement are out of phase)

READ is the corresponding verb. But STORY is both verb and noun; it can take continuative aspect – and when it does, it is interpreted as telling story after story, the verb interpretation.

Surprisingly, BULLSHIT and nondirectional B-S, which we just argued are nouns, can take continuative aspect, where the form of this aspectual marking exactly (to our eyes) coincides with the marking used on verbs. We use +++ to indicate movement features associated with continuative aspect in sentence (18), (see Figures 15 and 16).

(18)   HE {BULLSHIT-+++ / B-S-+++}.
         "He's bullshitting."

The senses of (18) range from "He's {just killing time/ not doing anything seriously},' to "He's {not trustworthy/ always bullshitting}." The sense of lying (rather than wasting time) is accompanied by slightly open pursed lips (as in playing a reed instrument) during the verbs BULLSHIT-+++/ B-S-+++ only, indicating slyness in the lying.

One might try to argue that in (18) we have nouns with the sense "characteristic bullshitter." However, this fails. NEVER can negate verbs but not nouns (Wilbur 1996) and NEVER can negate both BULLSHIT and nondirectional B-S, but only when they have +++, showing that they are verbs precisely only when they have the marker +++:

(19)   HE NEVER {BULLSHIT-+++/ B-S-+++}.
         "He never bullshits on and on."
         *HE NEVER {BULLSHIT/ B-S}.
         "He never bullshits."

Second, FINISH with the sense of a negative imperative can follow verbs but not nouns (Benedicto & Brentari 2004). Negative imperative FINISH can occur after BULLSHIT and nondirectional B-S when they have +++, but not otherwise, again showing they are verbs only when they have +++.

(20)   {BULLSHIT-+++/ B-S-+++} FINISH!
         "Stop bullshitting!"
         *{BULLSHIT/ B-S} FINISH!
         "Stop bullshitting!"

The examples we've given so far are single-clause sentences. However, BULLSHIT -+++ and nondirectional B-S-+++ can occur in complex sentences:

(21)   MAN INDEX$_i$ I SICK-OF INDEX$_i$ BULLSHIT-+++ NOT TRUST.
         "I'm sick of that man because he's always bullshitting; I don't trust him."

Here INDEX$_i$ indicates a spatial index, which the signer points to: in (21) the signer signs MAN, then points to a place in space, then signs I, then SICK-OF, then points to that same place in space, then signs BULLSHIT-+++, NOT, TRUST. In Section 4.2, we discuss diagnostics for sentence boundaries. For now, we note that none of those diagnostics occur in (21). So, BULLSHIT-+++ and nondirectional B-S-+++ can appear as embedded verbs, just like other verbs. The only thing special about these verbs is that they must have the +++ marker associated with continuative aspect.

What we have, then, are two nouns, BULLSHIT and nondirectional B-S, morphologically related to verbs that obligatorily have +++. Given that the N uses are familiar to all our consultants, whereas the V uses were brought up by our younger consultants and simply acknowledged by the older ones, we hypothesize that the derivation is N>V. The morphosyntactic behavior of the lexical items BULLSHIT and nondirectional B-S is unique in ASL. A range of verbs are derived from nouns (Supalla & Newport 1978; where nouns have shorter, repeated movement paths) and a range of nouns are derived from verbs (Klima & Bellugi 1979), but we know of no other derivation from noun to verb that requires a particular verbal marker on the resultant verb.

The pressing question is whether +++ indicates continuative aspect here, or is a derivational morpheme, turning Ns into Vs that just happens to be homophonous with the continuative aspect marker. One would want to avoid proliferation of homophonous verbal morphemes, particularly when +++ indicates continuative aspect when used with other Vs. But there is something about (18) that is different somehow from continuative aspect on a V and also on an adjective. In particular, if NOT is inserted in (18) preceding {BULLSHIT-+++/ B-S-+++}, the sense is "He's not just killing time" or "He's not bullshitting." Importantly, it does not mean "He's not a characteristic bullshitter." Indeed, he might well be a characteristic bullshitter, but that's not what is being remarked upon.

We believe what +++ adds to the V here is duration. That is, the subject didn't utter simply one bullshitty thing; he elaborated on it or he repeated it. It appears we have three uses of +++, then. One lends to an adjective a sense of characteristic behavior. One lends to a verb (most verbs, that is) the continuative aspect. And one lends to a denominal verb a sense of duration, where the only two denominal verbs we have encountered it with are BULLSHIT-+++ and nondirectional B-S-+++. Further, +++ is necessary to the denominal verb.

This should not be distressing; the requirement that a verb appear in a given aspect is not unheard of. Consider *shit*. With its literal sense, it can occur in any tense and/or aspect. But with its nonliteral meaning of "kid," it occurs only in progressive aspect (see [22a]). The only exception we know of is the sassy use of a sentence-final *not* with a first-person subject in the simple present tense (see [22b]):

(22)   a. He {is/ was} shitting you.
        *He {shits/ shat} you.
        b. I shit you not
        but: *I don't shit you.

Finally, we return to the agreeing verb B-S. For signers who have only the agreeing verb B-S, it does not co-occur with NONE (thus it would be ungrammatical in (15)), and, regardless of aspect, it can be negated with NEVER, can co-occur with the negative imperative FINISH, and can appear as an embedded verb (thus is it would be grammatical in (19), (20), and (21) with or without continuative aspect). In sum, it's unremarkable.

4.2 Predicates Taking Clauses as Their Arguments or as Modifiers

The bleached taboo-term predicates we present now often occur in final position of an utterance that contains another predicate. Are these final predicates a full sentence, an interjection, or part of a larger sentence with the string preceding them? Few diagnostics for syntactic structure aid in our analysis. Matters of binding cannot help because the argument structure of these predicates does not allow for syntactically telling binding opportunities.

However, prosody helps here. Phonological and syntactic constituents are not consistently isomorphic in sign languages any more than in speech (Nespor & Sandler 1999). Both modalities use prosodic structure to mark discourse function and emphasize constituents. Parentheticals, nonrestrictive relative clauses, topicalized elements, and extraposed elements form intonational phrases of their own in language after language (Sandler & Lillo-Martin 2006). However, the final intonational phrase and syntactic phrase of a sentence must coincide, so if there is no intonational phrase boundary between two lexical items, they belong to the same sentence (Fenlon et al. 2007; Ormel & Crasborn 2012).

While prosodic clues in sign language are encoded differently depending on sentence and signer (Wilbur & Martínez 2002), signers are sensitive to prosody. Intonational boundaries are indicated by multiple prosodic markers, at least two, but as many as eight, and typically blink is among them (Nicodemus 2009). Beyond blinks, these markers include changes in head position, body leans, length of signs, hand clasping, and changes in facial expression, such as eye aperture, cheek puffing, nose wrinkling (Tang et al. 2010). The absence of such markers between two lexical items indicates they belong to a single sentence.

Movement dynamics, however, are part of prosody and can change for emphasis. Emphasized signs use more proximal joints, with concomitant changes in dynamics (Mirus et al. 2001). Since emphasis is frequently present with taboo terms (even bleached ones), we expect to find an intonational phrase boundary preceding our taboo terms, even though they could well be within the same sentence as the sign preceding them. So, the absence of an intonational boundary between two elements indicates they are part of the same overall sentence, but the presence of such a boundary indicates nothing about sentencehood.

4.2.1 The Predicate GRUELING

Another sign our consultants offered moves bent-V (in Figure 17) from the side of the forehead to the side of the chin. We gloss it as GRUELING. This sign is not taboo, but when the topic of complaining, pejorative language came up in our data-gathering sessions, people offered it as an example. Perhaps it is best called slang (we have not found it in any dictionary).

We find GRUELING in (23):

Figure 17 GRUELING

(23)   a. I WORK-+++ ALL-NIGHT-LONG WOW GRUELING.
          "It's really awful that I (have to) keep working all night long."
          b. I WORK-+++ ALL-NIGHT-LONG CAN WOW GRUELING (CAN)).
          "It can be really awful that I (have to) keep working all night long."

WOW in (23) is an intensifier (similar to *way*: *That's way bad*); the hand shakes off to the side in neutral space, with thumb extended and the four fingers curved loosely. The sense of (23a) is that working all night long is grueling – hellish. And, while the subject of WORK-+++ ALL-NIGHT-LONG is coreferential with the signer here, it need not be. We contend that GRUELING in (23a) does not form its own utterance, but is instead a matrix predicate, predicating demandingness of the preceding clause. In support, Gaurav Mathur (personal communication, March 2011) pointed out that if we insert CAN, it will precede and, optionally, follow (WOW) GRUELING, as shown in (23b). Modals appear to the left of the verb they have scope over or at the end of that verb's clause, with differences in scope readings (Shaffer 2004). The ability of CAN to appear at all, as well as its particular location(s), show GRUELING is a predicate in (23).

Second, GRUELING cannot appear at the start of a conversation; (24) is ill-formed:

(24)   (A) *GRUELING!
          "It's really awful."
          (B) WHAT'S UP?
          "What's up?"
          (A) MY BOOK I LOST.
          "I lost my book."

But if in place of GRUELING we were to substitute the taboo finger gesture, or, for some signers, F-K, the discourse would work. So GRUELING does not stand on its own as an interjection.

GRUELING, however, can appear without a visually articulated preceding clause in the same utterance in other discourses:

(25)   (A) I WORK-+++ ALL-NIGHT-LONG.
        "I keep working all night long."
        (B) OH-YEAH? YOU HAPPY?
        "Oh, yeah? Are you happy (about that)?"
        (A) NO. GRUELING.
        "No. It's really awful."

Here we have a statement, then a response that asks about attitude toward that statement, and then a response with GRUELING, remarking on the event of working all night long. This is exactly the interpretation we expect if GRUELING has a phonetically null subject coreferential with the event of the already mentioned clause about working all night long. Indeed, GRUELING is always understood as predicated of an event.

Third, GRUELING occurs only when the preceding predicate is in continuative aspect. So, GRUELING puts constraints on that predicate, just as other predicates can put constraints on their sentential arguments.

Fourth, there is syntactic evidence that I WORK-+++ ALL-NIGHT-LONG is a subordinate clause. A subject tag can appear at the end of a sentence (simplex or complex), and must refer to the matrix clause subject (Padden 1988).

(26)   MOTHER INDEX$_i$ SINCE PERSUADE SISTER INDEX$_j$ COME INDEX$_i$.
        "My mother has been urging my sister to come and stay here, she (mother) has."
        *MOTHER INDEX$_i$ SINCE PERSUADE SISTER INDEX$_j$ COME INDEX$_j$
        "My mother has been urging my sister to come and stay here, she (sister) has."

Here the tag (the final INDEX) can be coreferential with the matrix subject, MOTHER, but not with the embedded subject, SISTER. If I WORK-+++ ALL-NIGHT-LONG were a matrix clause, we'd expect that the subject tag "I" could be added either after ALL-NIGHT-LONG (if GRUELING were not part of the overall sentence) or at the end. However, it cannot appear in either position.

As further evidence that (23) is a single sentence, in our videotape of (23) none of the elements that optionally mark intonational phrase boundaries occur between ALL-NIGHT-LONG and WOW, nor between WOW and GRUELING, with one exception: mouth shape. The mouth forms a tight O starting at the end of ALL-NIGHT-LONG and extending across both WOW and GRUELING. However, that mouth movement is lexically associated with the sign WOW, and might be perseverative with respect to GRUELING. There is no other nonmanual change at this point in the sentence. In fact, the facial expressions are distinct beginning with ALL-NIGHT-LONG and carrying through unchanged onto WOW and GRUELING. So ALL-NIGHT-LONG, WOW, and GRUELING are part of a single intonational phrase.

The only syntactic analysis of (23) consistent with its semantics and syntactic behavior has GRUELING as the matrix predicate. Again, we see a structure not argued for elsewhere in the literature. Sentential subjects in ASL have been proposed, but when it comes to predicates that take clauses as their sole argument, they are clause-initial scene setters (SEEM, HAPPEN, TEND, etc.; see Napoli & Sutton-Spence 2021). In contrast, GRUELING is fully fledged predicative, and it comes clause-finally.

4.2.2 The Predicate FUCK-IT

Another type of bleached taboo predicate is found in FUCK-IT: the taboo finger gesture jabs toward an object within view or toward an indexed point in space, or, sometimes, toward neutral space. If the videophone is flashing, one might do FUCK-IT toward the phone to show they're not going to bother answering it. So, FUCK-IT is an agreeing verb. The dissociation asserted need not cast aspersions. That is, the handshape itself is not vulgar; for many, it occurs in the non-taboo signs TANK (handspeak.com) and the Washington, DC slang sign for MONUMENT (www.washingtonpost.com/express/wp/2014/12/15/d-c-has-its-own-sign-language-slang/). The jabbing motion makes FUCK-IT vulgar.

We argue that FUCK-IT is a predicate that can take a sentential argument: the subject dissociates themself from a particular object or event. While the subject of FUCK-IT need not be coreferential with the signer, the signer's body represents the subject (Meir et al. 2007). FUCK-IT, then, takes an ordinary subject (embodied by the signer) and an object that is either an NP or sentential. One might use FUCK-IT to say that John dissociates himself from the phone or from some event (maybe that the refrigerator is empty). Importantly, if the thing to be dissociated from is abstract, agreement need not occur; one can simply jab toward neutral space, as in Figure 18, which could be used in a sentence such as:

(27)   LOVE FUCK-IT
        "I can't be bothered with love."

Figure 18 FUCK-IT

The use of FUCK-IT of interest to us appears in final position of complex sentences, as in:

(28)   <u>   br   </u>
STUDY FRENCH FUCK-IT.
"I can't be bothered with studying French."

The line above STUDY FRENCH with the label br indicates that eyebrows are raised during these two signs, marking this intonational phrase as a topic (Wilbur & Patschke 1999). So, the clause STUDY FRENCH is an embedded clause. The only other lexical element here is FUCK-IT, so FUCK-IT is the predicate. In (28) the agreement verb FUCK-IT points toward neutral space. This is not disturbing, since the topic clause is abstract and, as we noted, FUCK-IT may point toward neutral space when it takes an object (here topic) that is abstract, as in (27). Further, clauses do not have a spatial index, so there is no spatial index available for FUCK-IT to agree with.

Many verbs have been argued to take sentential objects (THINK, WANT, EXPECT, etc.). But FUCK-IT is remarkable when it comes to agreement. Consider:

(29)   <u>   br   </u>
THAT$_i$ CLASS NOT TAKE AGAIN FUCK-IT$_i$
"I can't be bothered with taking that class again."

Again, the sentence begins with a topic, this time an NP. But, in contrast to (28), it is not clear that (29) is a complex sentence, rather than two sentences (with a sentence boundary after AGAIN). For the moment, let's assume (29) has an analysis as a complex sentence in order to discuss why it is of interest. Then we defend this analysis (arguing that (29) has two pronunciations – where the complex-sentence reading is represented in the translation here).

In (29) the subjects of the two clauses are coreferential. So, FUCK-IT conveys its subject's decision to dissociate herself from the event of taking that class again. The surprising fact is that instead of FUCK-IT pointing toward neutral space, as it does in (28), FUCK-IT in (29) agrees with the spatial index of THAT, as indicated by our referential indices. This agreement fact does not correlate to any new complexity of interpretation. That is, while FUCK-IT is inflected for agreement with an entity inside the preceding clause, we understand the subject to be dissociating herself from the event of taking the class. The subject might, in fact, have enjoyed the class (so she's not dissociating herself from the class), but for whatever reason taking it again is not on the agenda.

In other comparably complex constructions, our consultants likewise allow FUCK-IT to agree with an entity within a preceding clause or to point to neutral space. When conveying the proposition "Noriko woke up sick this morning and decided not to go to work," the ASL construction could end with WORK FUCK-IT, and the middle finger of FUCK-IT could point toward the location in space where the sign WORK was made, or toward the site of working (if the actual site was located over to one side of the signer or if that site had been spatially indexed in the conversation), or toward neutral space.

These agreement facts are startling. And, of course, they depend on a complex-sentence analysis of (29), which is tricky precisely because the string of signs in (29) can be articulated in two ways. One is with a sentence boundary after AGAIN; the other is without such a boundary (reflected in our translation of [29]). As two sentences, a better translation of (29) would be "I'm not going to take that class again. I can't be bothered (with it)." With that reading, we find an intonational phrase boundary after AGAIN (marked with multiple nonmanual changes), and a subject tag can appear at the end of either sentence, and finally complete additional sentences can intervene between the two. In (30) (offered to us by an anonymous referee), the first sentence has a final subject tag, then a long sentence intervenes before we get to the FUCK-IT sentence:

(30)   THAT CLASS NOT TAKE AGAIN, WON'T I. SAME-OVER-AND-OVER, BORING, DON'T LIKE. FUCK-IT.
"I won't take that class again. It's the same thing over and over, it's boring. I don't like it.
I can't be bothered with it."

With the complex-sentence reading given in (29), instead, we have no intonational phrase boundary after AGAIN. Our consultants produced this reading with a negative facial expression on AGAIN that carried over, without other intonational phrase boundary markers, onto FUCK-IT. So, both prosodic information and semantics support a complex-sentence analysis beside the two-sentence analysis.

We account now for the agreement of FUCK-IT with an element inside its object complement in the complex-sentence reading of (29). Since FUCK-IT usually agrees with its object, and since it is impossible to mark it for agreement with an entire clause, the default is to mark it for agreement with some appropriate lexical item within its sentential object, or with some appropriate real location (such as a nearby worksite), although, again, one could choose to simply point it toward neutral space. Once more, we have a new syntactic phenomenon in these unique agreement details. This looks like a metonymic mapping (somewhat similar to agreement with a single index that represents a group; see Mathur and Rathmann 2010).

Figure 19 FUCK-EVERYTHING/EVERYONE

4.2.3 The Predicate FUCK-EVERYTHING/EVERYONE

A third kind of bleached taboo predicate also uses the taboo finger gesture: FUCK-EVERYTHING/EVERYONE (a literal gloss; the sense is "ignore"). The hands start close together, palms oriented upward, with the middle fingers nearly crossing. Wrists rotate outward as hands move apart and rise (Figure 19).

This verb can occur with a clause following it:

(31)   NIGHT FUCK-EVERYTHING/EVERYONE STUDY ALL-NIGHT-LONG.
         "Tonight I'm ignoring everything/everyone because I'm going to study all night long."

We first argue that (31) is a single complex sentence, then discuss its structure. In two out of three video recordings of (31), no nonmanuals changed between FUCK-EVERYTHING/EVERYONE and STUDY. In the third video recording, mouth position changed, but nothing else (in particular, no blink). Since an intonational phrase boundary is a necessary but not sufficient indication of a sentence boundary, there is a reading of (31) in which FUCK-EVERYTHING/EVERYONE and STUDY are part of one complex sentence.

(31) tells us that studying is the reason why I am ignoring everything. So, we have a matrix predicate, FUCK-EVERYTHING/EVERYONE, modified by a sentence-initial time adverbial (NIGHT) and a following adverbial clause of reason (STUDY ALL-NIGHT-LONG). Most adverbial clauses in ASL occur in initial position of the matrix clause (Wilbur 2016). The only adverbial clauses that come on the "right" side that we know of are those introduced by UNDERSTAND (Fischer & Lillo-Martin 1990). So, our discussion of FUCK-EVERYTHING/EVERYONE will hopefully motivate further investigation of adverbial clauses that come at the end of the matrix clause.

Figure 20 RECIPROCAL-FUCK-OFF

4.3 Verb Strings

The final bleached taboo predicate we study here has both hands in the taboo finger gesture as they jab toward each other: RECIPROCAL-FUCK-OFF, as shown in Figure 20.

RECIPROCAL-FUCK-OFF can be used as the only verb in a sentence with the meaning "don't get along/ aren't on speaking terms/ always quarrel." But it can also appear in a sentence with another verb, as in:

(32)   THE-TWO-OF-THEM NOT GET-ALONG RECIPROCAL-FUCK-OFF
       "The two of them don't get along at all."

Given the reading of (32), one might think that RECIPROCAL-FUCK-OFF is not a verb, but perhaps a modifier, emphasizing NOT GET-ALONG. While it does have that force, it is syntactically a verb with the sense of each showing a fuck-you attitude toward the other. Like with other reciprocal verbs, if we change the subject from THE-TWO-OF-THEM to THE-THREE-OF-THEM, the result is ungrammatical:

(33)   * THE-THREE-OF-THEM NOT GET-ALONG RECIPROCAL-FUCK-OFF
       "The three of them don't get along at all."

RECIPROCAL-FUCK-OFF imposes a sense of the subject being precisely two entities: (34) means precisely two families do not get along.

(34)   THOSE FAMILIES NOT GET-ALONG RECIPROCAL-FUCK-OFF.
       "Those (two) families do not get along at all."

The syntactic structure of (32) is a puzzle. The prosody shows it is a single sentence, where THE-TWO-OF-THEM forms its own intonational phrase and the following string forms another. Additionally, there are three syntactic arguments that (32) is a single sentence. First, AND cannot be inserted before RECIPROCAL-FUCK-OFF in (32), although AND can occur between separate sentences (given appropriate pragmatics) and between conjoined clauses (Padden 1988).

(35)   *THE-TWO-OF-THEM NOT GET-ALONG AND RECIPROCAL-FUCK-OFF
         "The two of them don't get along and they want nothing to do with each other."

Second, we cannot have an indexical (indicating the two of them) inserted before RECIPROCAL-FUCK-OFF in (32), although that's where an indexical subject could appear if we had separate sentences or conjoined clauses. In (36) the IX indicates an indexical spatially coindexed with THE-TWO-OF-THEM.

(36)   *THE-TWO-OF-THEM$_i$ NOT GET-ALONG IX$_i$ RECIPROCAL-FUCK-OFF
         "The two of them don't get along; they want nothing to do with each other."

However, (36) is good with an intonational break after GET-ALONG. So, the grammaticality of (36) depends on having two sentences, not one. Third, normally full sentences and conjoined clauses can be reversed in order without changing the meaning so long as issues of chronology don't enter. However, while we can reverse the order of the verbs in (32), the sense is affected:

(37)   THE-TWO-OF-THEM RECIPROCAL-FUCK-OFF NOT GET-ALONG.
         "The two of them want nothing to do with each other. They don't get along."

(37) is grammatical with the sense given there. But that is not the sense of (32). In (32), RECIPROCAL-FUCK-OFF remarks on how strongly they don't get along. So (37) is most probably two sentences.

All evidence leads to the conclusion that (32) is a single sentence. But what is its structure? Neither of the predicates in (32) takes a clause as an argument: there is no subordination here. We also do not have a compound verb here, since RECIPROCAL-FUCK-OFF can occur independently from GET-ALONG. In (32), other verbs that might be substituted for GET-ALONG include KISS and HUG. If we remove NOT, additional verbs could be substituted, such as ARGUE or GLARE-AT-EACH-OTHER. So, we have two separate, unconjoined verbs in (32).

We conclude we have a two-verb string in a single clause. Serial verbs in many spoken languages also involve strings of verbs that share the same subject without being subordinated or coordinated to the other. An example from Thai (Muansuwan 2001: 229) is:

(38)   Malee **wîŋ troŋ jɔɔn khâam** saphaan **ʔɔɔk paj**
         Malee run go-straight reverse cross bridge exit go
         "Malee ran straight back, crossing the bridge, away from the speaker."

Sign languages also exhibit serial verb constructions (Benedicto, Cvejanov & Quer 2008): the two verbs are linearly nonseparable and share an argument. Is (32) a serial verb construction?

While the verb string in (32) is similar to serial verb strings, differences appear. For one, in serial verb constructions in spoken languages, often the first verb modifies the next. In sign language serial verb constructions, instead, neither verb emphasizes or modifies the other, but together they give more comprehensive information about a single action. In sentences like (32), however, the second verb (RECIPROCAL-FUCK-OFF) emphasizes the first verb: we have a third kind of interaction of semantics between the two predicates. Another difference is that in serial verb constructions in spoken and sign languages, the first verb belongs to a small semantic set, such as verbs of motion, giving, or taking. Generally, the first verb is semantically closely tied to the second verb, together describing a single overall event. In sign languages this relationship is further constrained: the first verb is a manner of motion and the other is a path verb. But with RECIPROCAL-FUCK-OFF the action of the first verb and that of the second are unrelated in type. What ties the two verbs together is that the first should be an action typical of people showing disregard for each other.

At this point, it looks like (32) is an example of a previously unnoticed type of serial verb construction. However, negation distinguishes (32) from serial verb constructions. In serial verb constructions in spoken language a negative has scope over all verbs. And in serial verb constructions in sign languages negatives don't appear. In contrast, in constructions with RECIPROCAL-FUCK-OFF, a negative can appear on the first verb without having scope over the second verb: in (32) NOT has scope over GET-ALONG but not over RECIPROCAL-FUCK-OFF.

In sum, we have in (32) a single clause with two verbs where the second emphasizes the first, but it is not clear that this is a serial verb construction. Either our picture of serial verb constructions needs to be enriched in the ways we've indicated here, or we have stumbled across a new syntactic relationship.

4.4 Concluding Remarks

Bleached taboo-term predicates give evidence for syntactic structures in ASL that have not yet been argued for. Some of these predicates exhibit unique grammatical behavior. We've seen conversion of nouns into verbs (but always with the +++ marker, as in BULLSHIT and nondirectional B-S), a predicate that takes a sentential subject (GRUELING) but is not presentational, an agreement verb that takes a sentential object and agrees in an unusual way (FUCK-IT), a verb that takes a modifying clause following it (FUCK-EVERYTHING/EVERYONE), and a verb string that involves neither conjoining nor embedding, but is distinct from serial verb strings in some ways (with RECIPROCAL-FUCK-OFF). This last construction might be new not just in the analysis of ASL, but in the analysis of language in general.

5 (Sub)Lexical Changes in Iconic Signs to Realign with Community Sensibilities and Experiences

Iconicity in sign language lexicons is frequent and ranges across a wide range of visually perceived characteristics of objects. Over time, the referents of these lexical items can fall out of use, such as for reasons of technological or environmental change, resulting in a misalignment of form and sense. That misalignment might be tolerated or might lead to variants with (sub)lexical changes that realign form and sense. Often corrections of this sort involve taboo topics or terms, and, thus, might be open to an analysis as euphemisms – a mistake, as we will argue.

5.1 Background

Alongside studies of taboo terms in spoken languages are studies of euphemism (e.g., *let go* for *fired*). Some studies look at how euphemisms change over time (Linfoot-Ham 2005); others examine the range of linguistic mechanisms employed in euphemisms (McGlone, Beck & Pfiester 2006).

In speech, a common means of avoiding taboo terms while still getting across taboo ideas is circumlocution. This occurs in sign languages as well: RESTROOM exists side-by-side with TOILET in ASL. Some circumlocutions are simply sounds (*Where is the ehum?*). In ASL a comparable circumlocution might involve nonmanuals, such as head tilted back, close-lipped smile, blinks, upward gaze, or a combination. Sometimes circumlocutions involve metaphors (*passed (on)* for *die*). Sign languages likewise use metaphors, such as ABSENT/ GONE for "die," which can occur alone but is frequently in a compound, such as that meaning "widow": HUSBAND^GONE.

Another euphemism strategy is to disguise taboo expressions by using written conventions. In spoken languages, this is done via acronyms (*snafu* for "situation normal all fucked up") and abbreviations (*Why don't you just F-off now?*). Sign languages, likewise, appropriate writing via initialization (B-S for "bullshit"), which typically does not, however, reduce offensiveness. Additionally, sign languages appropriate writing via fingerspelling, which can be euphemistic. For example, in ASL s-L-U-T is a euphemistic option to SLUT, according to our consultants. Still, some signs are always fingerspelled and retain their taboo status: D-O-U-C-H-E-B-A-G.

Finally, euphemisms can involve phonetic changes (*shoot* vs. *shit*). Sign languages can do this, as well; in ASL SHIT is articulated with the thumb of the dominant hand moving out of what can be seen as the bottom of an enclosure formed by the nondominant hand, while a less offensive variant has the thumb going into the top of that enclosure.

5.2 Sex-Related Signs and Euphemism

Early mentions of euphemism in sign languages note variation in signs regarding sexual activities or sex-related body parts (Woodward 1979). Pyers (2006) notes that indexical pointing signs are frequent for some body parts (eyes, nose), but pointing to genitals is impolite, hence the existence of lexical signs for genitalia. Pointing directs the eyes, and looking toward someone's genitals is rude in most situations. This is a subtle kind of euphemism, one that might not have a counterpart in speech – the euphemism of avoiding leading the addressee toward inappropriate behavior. Sutton-Spence and Woll (1999) suggest for British Sign Language that euphemism can be achieved via reducing visual explicitness, including changing sign location. Likewise, Loos, Cramer, and Napoli (2019) show that degree of offensiveness in German Sign Language is affected by changes in phonological parameters.

Sze, Wei, and Wong (2017) set the groundwork for broad studies of euphemism in sign. They look at the sign languages of Hong Kong, Jakarta, Sri Lanka (SLSL), and Japan, to determine whether euphemisms in sex-related signs are geared toward lowering the visual iconicity of the sign – which they do, indeed, conclude, giving examples of phonological change. A fascinating finding is the euphemism strategy of replacing manual phonological parameters with strictly nonmanual articulation. For example, "menstruation" in SLSL can be conveyed via repeated lower-lip biting. This can be done in spoken language, as in, *You know she's* . . . where the " . . . " is filled with a depictive facial gesture indicating a variety of things (such as mental illness). Sze and colleagues further found that the addition of a nonmanual parameter can make an inoffensive term highly taboo.

5.3 Corrections

Often changes in culture lead to the original sense of a word no longer being pertinent to the situations in which one would have ordinarily used it. Such situations need not concern taboo. Technological change, for example, often wreaks havoc with lexical sense. Today most cameras record digitally, yet we

Figure 21 ASL older sign SHAVE

Figure 22 ASL newer sign SHAVE

still speak of the "film" industry. Sometimes, however, speakers do not tolerate misnomers. Records were replaced by cassette tapes, then CDs, then DVDs – with lexical items coined for new objects.

Misnomers arise in sign languages, as well, frequently due to the possibility of iconicity. The older verb SHAVE in Figure 21 (lifeprint.com), is iconic of when one used a straight edge razor (the Y shows the span of the blade). The newer verb in Figure 22 (lifeprint.com), is iconic of a modern electric or disposable-cartridge razor (the X shows a smaller surface touching the face).

Technology changed; the lexicon caught up by changing the handshape; hence, a correction. But the English word *shave* presents no alignment of form and meaning, so differences in the blade that touches the skin do not result in conundrums for speakers. Not all misalignments in signs are handled with corrections, however. ASL signers often use both older and newer variants of all the signs in this section: corrections are a tendency, not an absolute.

For example, the word *telephone* has persisted in English since the first device of that type. The situation in ASL differs. The older sign TELEPHONE in Figure 23a (www.youtube.com/watch?v=jhM_dZHjjas) appears beside the newer sign in Figure 23b (lifeprint.com), which is used more often than the newest sign in Figure 23 c (lifeprint.com). The sign in Figure 23a is iconic of

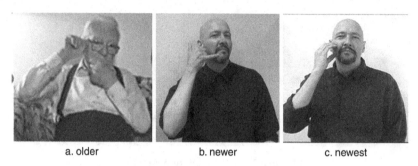

a. older   b. newer   c. newest

Figure 23 ASL signs TELEPHONE

telephones that had two parts, for listening and for speaking. Those disappeared when dial phones with handsets came in. Accordingly, the older sign was replaced by newer signs. The sign in Figure 23b is iconic of the handset. The other newer sign in Figure 23c simply has a C-handshape at the ear – and it refers only to mobile phones. Nevertheless, the variant in Figure 23b persists, despite the rarity of handset/dial telephones today.

Signers have not corrected the misalignment in TELEPHONE in Figure 23b, perhaps because that sign is considered to have an arbitrary relationship of form to meaning. In support of that possibility, note that the sign in Figure 23b is an agreeing verb: it is not locked in position. One could sign the sense "I telephone my friend," for example, by moving the Y in Figure 23b from the signer's face out toward a location in space that has been indexed for my friend. Once the handshape is no longer located on the face, its iconicity (all but) disappears.

What makes one misalignment tolerated while another calls for correction? Our contention is that misalignments can be tolerated (although need not be) so long as they are not regrettable, where sources of regret are misalignments concerning matters of particular relevance or importance to deaf experience. If tolerable misalignments are maintained, the relationship between form and meaning becomes arbitrary over time, and eventually the misalignment is no longer perceived (e.g., TELEPHONE in Figure 23b). With regrettable misalignments, however, the relationship between form and meaning acts as a persistent irritant – hence they tend to be corrected. It is that feeling of "wrong" that we are tipping our hat to when we dub these changes "corrections."

Judging what is particularly relevant or important to deaf experience is sometimes easy. CALL-BY-TTY changed over time. The original sign was the sign for TELEPHONE in Figure 23b followed by the sign TYPE. It was replaced by simply T-T-Y. So, the lexical item for the machine that was used by deaf people (TTY) was regrettable and changed so that it would not clash with deaf experiences, while the lexical item for the machine that was not used by deaf people

Figure 24 ASL sign VIDEOPHONE

(handset/dial telephone) didn't change. When relay services and other modern alternatives came in, many adopted other signs for these newer modes, such as F-T for FaceTime calls, and the sign in Figure 24 (signingsavvy.com) for VIDEOPHONE.

Other times, however, judging what is particularly relevant or important calls for profound understanding of deaf experience, and, since deaf experience varies, can lead to controversy over lexical change. In Sections 5.3.1 and 5.3.2, we offer two common types of regrettable misalignments that have fueled heated discussion among our consultants and on the Internet. One type concerns respect for identities and often involves (sometimes bleached) taboos; the other type concerns being true to deaf experiences. In both types of misalignments, the regrettable part is founded on the nature and role of language itself in the lives of deaf people.

The unique situation of deaf people vis-à-vis language is a key-player in the determination of whether a misalignment of form and meaning is regrettable, and, hence of whether correction is in order. Many signers are invested in whether their language reflects realities and truths as they know them – witness discussions on websites such as the Facebook group ASL THAT! and audismfreeamerica.blogspot.com. They debate whether existing signs need modification or replacement and who has the right to make such correction, as well as who has the right to coin signs. They compare sign languages to minority spoken languages and they express alliance with oppressed minorities.

5.3.1 Correction Based on Recognition of and Respect for Identity

Language regarding identities is often the subject of controversy among hearing people, sometimes leading to lexical changes. A number of scholars have studied functional diversity with respect to identity issues and have looked at ways of referring to those identities/groups, sometimes with at least passing attention to euphemism (Muredda 2012), where many of the examples that come up involve replacing explicitness with vagueness (e.g., talking about children with "special needs"; see Back and colleagues 2016).

Sometimes politically correct (PC) efforts prevail; outsiders can police language and "reform" on "behalf" of an oppressed community. This can result in a term falling out use. Occasionally, sublexical changes are proposed and spread (witness *latinx* on university campuses). But not always. Galvin (2003: 155) notes that PC language often fails in resisting oppressive identifications because "if the concepts behind the words remain unchanged, then the new words end up being just as negative in their connotations." Halmari (2011) suggests that sometimes new wording then becomes oppressive, leading to the desire for further euphemisms or lexical innovations.

When we turn to sign languages, we sometimes find iconic signs that identify groups, where the graphics zero in on a visually identifiable characteristic. That characteristic, however, might not be how the group views itself nor how it wants others to view it. Empathy with that group can lead outsiders to see the label as incorrect; they perceive a misalignment of form with meaning. For example, the older ASL sign for CHINA involves touching the corner of the eye, whereas the newer sign is borrowed from Chinese Sign Language (and involves touching the torso in a backwards 7-path) and the older ASL sign ITALY involves drawing a cross on the forehead, whereas the newer sign is borrowed from Italian Sign Language (and involves outlining a peninsula). The concern here is less one of trying to avoid offense and more one of trying to correct a sign based on an identification that doesn't ring true.

Correction often takes the form of modifying the phonology to obliterate the misalignment. Many examples of correction regarding identity concern minority groups, where something about the group touches on traditional ideas of taboo. People with disabilities or serious illnesses are included here, as are those with sexual behaviors other than straight and monogamous. The older sign BLIND in Figure 25a (www.signingsavvy.com) moves bent-V directly toward the eyes, while one newer variant of BLIND in Figure 25b (https://aslsignbank .haskins.yale.edu/dictionary/gloss/2117) moves that handshape toward the ipsilateral cheek below the eye, and another new variant of BLIND moves the handshape toward a much lower point on the face (as in the version on www

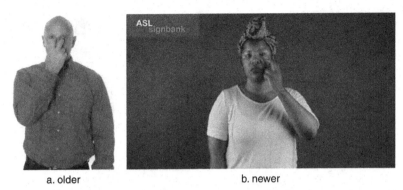

a. older   b. newer

Figure 25 ASL sign BLIND

Figure 26 ASL sign SEE

.handspeak.com). Vision is alluded to in the V-handshape itself (indicating two eyes; perhaps originally an initialization from French *voir* "see"), but the location correction to the cheek or lower adds arbitrariness, in line with the perception that blindness, as an identity, involves more than lack of sight.

One might object that the change in Figure 25 is simply phonological. After all, location variation can be conditioned by phonological factors (Lucas et al. 2002). And a likely phonological account presents itself: the shift in location could be an example of the diachronic tendency to move signs from the center to the perimeter of the face (Frishberg 1975). In fact, the ASL sign SEE is at the perimeter of the face, not the center, as in Figure 26 (www.lifeprint.com).

In opposition to a phonological account, we compare the change in location in BLIND to the location of DOUBT. The handshape in both is the same. For some signers, DOUBT moves the hand away and back in front of the eyes, as in

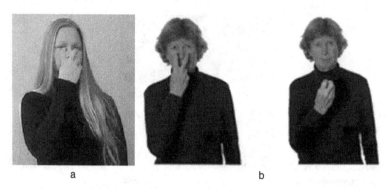

a   b

Figure 27 Two variants of ASL sign DOUBT

Figure 27a (www.aslpro.com). For others, DOUBT moves the hand from below the eyes outward and downward – sometimes curling the fingers tightly as the hand moves away, as in Figure 27b (www.signingsavvy.com). Both variations start with the hand central to the face.

These variants of DOUBT and the older variant of BLIND (Figure 25a) are phonologically similar, the major difference being that the initial movement in BLIND is toward the face and the initial movement in DOUBT is away. But it is only in a newer variant of BLIND, not in any variant of DOUBT, that location has shifted from the center of the face to the periphery. Thus, while the lowering of the hand in the variant of BLIND on www.handspeak.com might simply be phonological (by the same process that lowers the hand in one newer variant of DOUBT), the shift to the side of the face in another new variant of BLIND in Figure 25b most probably is not. Diachronic change in sign languages is not regular in the way that change in spoken languages is (Moser 1990). Nevertheless, the contrast between the variants in Figure 27 and the newer form in Figure 25b make a correction account of the change in BLIND likely.

We have already noted the frequent use of change of location as a strategy for euphemisms (Section 5.2). Could the change in Figure 25 be an example of euphemism, not correction? Our consultants tell us that the newer sign in Figure 25b isn't polite or nice (as euphemisms are), but, rather, sensible and more in line with what we know about the complexity of identities.

The motivation for the newer sign in Figure 25b might also be political, in the sense of deaf people being allies to blind people. Many deaf people express opposition to being defined by audiological status alone; that definition has led to a devaluation of deaf cultures and lives (Bauman 2008). Our consultants tell us they do not want to be guilty of perpetrating the same harm on blind people.

Correction is a way of setting the story straight – whether with regard to a changing technology, experience, or sensibility. Rather than continue with

a. older   b. newer

Figure 28 ASL sign LESBIAN

a range of lexical items that were coined without empathy, often by an out-group for whom the older lexical items might be self-serving, people change the lexicon to reflect their own understandings of the world.

Another example regarding identity of a minority group is variation for LESBIAN. Kleinfeld and Warner (1996) note four variants. In two older variants, the web between thumb and index finger of the L-handshape contacts the chin. In the other two, the tip of the index finger contacts either the area under the contralateral corner of the mouth or the chin. Figure 28 shows an older (www .youtube.com/watch?v=TknYwESRjDo) and a newer (www.youtube.com /watch?v=jTdCZ9i1WY8) variant.

It could be that LESBIAN was originally arbitrary – where L is an initialization and the contact point was random (just as GAY makes a G on the chin). However, folk etymologies attribute iconicity, and appear to have a kind of collective reality in sign languages just as they have in spoken languages. One of our consultants volunteered the interpretation of the older form as L representing spread legs, so Figure 28a is iconic of oral sex. Others saw that L as iconic of genitals (consistent with the fact that two Ls come together in the sign VAGINA, as the signer in Figure 28b says). Some signers play with the older variant in a mocking way by sticking out the tongue and flicking it. Nyle DiMarco (DiMarco & Man 2018) asserts that the older sign is to be eschewed, and the newer form is respectful. Our consultants agree. The change in point of contact may be a correction; a lesbian identity concerns more than engaging in a sexual act.

Again, we consider the possibility that the variation might not be a correction, but, instead, due to the phonological tendency to move signs away from the center of the face (which, here, is an effect of changing the point of contact from web between thumb and index finger to tip of index finger). In response, we offer first the fact that our consultants as well as web sources (Greene 2011) indicate that the newer form is preferred because the older form reveals a lack of

Figure 29 ASL sign LUNCH

Figure 30 ASL sign TRANSSEXUAL

understanding of sexuality and gender. Second, the tendency to move away from the center of the face does not appear to apply to signs made on the chin (BITCH, BREAKFAST, FINLAND, JEWISH, LUNCH, DINNER, PREFER, SWEET, WRONG). LUNCH in Figure 29 (lifeprint.com) uses L just like LESBIAN does, though the orientation is different (the palm faces contralateral), which leads to a different contact (thumb tip touches the chin). So, we have a near minimal pair here. A purely phonological account based on the tendency to move away from the center of the face, then, is suspect.

An anonymous reviewer suggested considering a different phonological account, one based on change in point of contact. However, while there are, indeed, few signs in ASL in which the web of the dominant hand moves to make contact with some other body location (as in BUTTERFLY or BRACELET), we know of no tendency to change point of contact from web to any other part of the hand. Further, some signers make contact of that web in at least two other signs located on the chin, both using O>S (where for other signers the radial side of the hand is used): ORANGE and OLD.

A third example of correction based on recognition of identity involves lexical substitution. Here, the older and newer sign rely on a sign-internal change in palm orientation. TRANSSEXUAL originally had the X-handshape contact the ipsilateral

Figure 31 ASL sign TRANSGENDER

a. older   b. newer

Figure 32 ASL signs COME-OUT

cheek, palm oriented away from the signer (as in SEX), then the forearm rotated (by radioulnar articulation), so that the palm was oriented toward the signer, as in Figure 30 (www.youtube.com/watch?v=0Qpo58kJCYU):

For many, this sign has been replaced by one better glossed as TRANSGENDER: 5, with palm oriented contralaterally, touches the chest and closes to a flat-O while radioulnar movement changes palm orientation, as shown in Figure 31 (https://www.youtube.com/watch?v=Byuw-A5Srts).

DiMarco and Man (2018) offer a folk history; Man proposes the sign BEAUTIFUL moved from face to chest (i.e., a transgender person is claiming internal beauty). Shannon (2017), instead, sees the newer sign as taking what is inside the chest – inner identity – and turning it outward, so others can see it. Either interpretation is a correction; transgender people make a change not defined by sexuality alone.

A fourth example involving identity replaces a sign, where articulatory characteristics of the newer and older signs have nothing in common. An older COME-OUT in Figure 32a (SignSchool 2016a) mimics opening a coat; a newer sign in Figure 32b (SignSchool 2016b) has X unhook and move "out of" the nondominant hand. The older version is taken by some as insulting gay people because it brings to mind exposing genitalia (Kleinfeld & Warner 1996: 17; although many deaf people in the LGBTQ community use it without insult). The newer term recognizes coming out as a detachment; one of our consultants suggested it is a metaphor for getting off the "vehicle" that was carrying you along till now.

5.3.2 Correction Based on Deaf Experiences

Often expressions in sign differ from comparably used expressions in ambient spoken languages in a way appropriate to deaf experiences. These expressions need not concern taboo. ASL PAY-ATTENTION in Figure 33 (https://aslsignbank .haskins.yale.edu/dictionary/gloss/213/) is iconic of directing visual attention.

Other times, a sign expression stems from an expression in the ambient spoken language that has little to do with deaf experience. ASL has SOUND +LIKE in Figure 34 (www.signingsavvy.com), as in *Sounds like you're unhappy.*

This kind of example is common (cf., SOUND+GOOD), and, generally, our consultants don't seem to notice the inappropriateness. That may be due to the nature of it being a fixed phrase, thus, understood holistically, not componentially.

On the other hand, there are instances in which the inappropriateness is problematic. LISTEN has at least two forms. One means "pay attention to audible information" – articulated at the ear, as in Figure 35 (https://aslsignbank

Figure 33 ASL sign PAY-ATTENTION

Figure 34 ASL sign SOUND+LIKE

Figure 35 ASL sign LISTEN or older sign for RECEIVE-INFORMATION/PERCEIVE

Figure 36 ASL newer sign LISTEN/PERCEIVE

.haskins.yale.edu/dictionary/gloss/478). It is often used to mean "receive information generally."

A newer variant means, instead, "receive information" and is articulated on the cheek under the eye, often with the nondominant hand also articulating in neutral space, as in Figure 35 (https://aslsignbank.haskins.yale.edu/dictionary/gloss/213). The change from an older location incongruous with deaf experiences, in Figure 35, to a new location congruent with deaf experiences, in Figure 36, is a correction.

Another example concerns POETRY. The older sign differs from MUSIC only by handshape; MUSIC uses B and POETRY uses P, in Figure 37 (www .signingsavvy.com). The older sign draws a parallel between music and poetry via initialization that might not be congruous with deaf experiences.

The newer sign in Figure 38 (www.youtube.com/watch?v=xRcwVRf5BS8) is a lexical substitution. The hand moves up the chest, turns over (via radioulnar movement), then moves forward and down. The iconicity is of taking something from inside oneself and pulling it up and out to offer to the addressee. Peter Cook and Kenny Lerner (Flying Words Project 2008) in the poem "Poetry" explain that poetry is a relationship between the poet's heart and the outside.

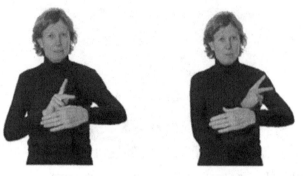

Figure 37 ASL older sign POETRY

Figure 38 ASL newer sign POETRY

Figure 39 ASL older sign INTERSECTIONALITY

The newer sign's articulation is more appropriate to deaf experience: this substitution is a correction.

The examples here may bring to mind debates about language colonialism and linguistic hegemony, where spoken language would be the bully. It is not our intention to feed those fires. In fact, we find corrections regarding congruity with deaf experiences in signs that have nothing to do with spoken language. These signs are originally coined by deaf communities and are partially changed or replaced as experiences change. Figure 39 (www.youtube.com/watch? v=DdurIuHyWaA) presents one older variant of INTERSECTIONALITY. The hands come together (fingers wiggling) until one is on top, they settle downward and stop with a hold, iconic of overlapping identities.

In one newer variant that some of our consultants adopt (from www .handspeak.com), the hands start with fingers interlaced and they move together, iconic of linked identities that act together (despite the fact that they are sometimes in opposition) without suggestion of one being a base upon which others are overlaid. None of the many variants for INTERSECTIONALITY was imposed by or derived from speech; but correction is happening as knowledge about intersectionality grows.

5.4 Concluding Remarks

When the relationship between form and sense is nonarbitrary, a lexical item's articulation can become inappropriate. If that inappropriateness is a misalignment of a community's knowledge of how self and the world works, that is, if it feels wrong, then (sub)lexical change might occur to bring about a realignment that corrects it, particularly if the inappropriateness is offensive.

Correction realignment is distinct from euphemism, circumlocution, or phonetic change that disguises a taboo topic. Unlike PC, its primary goal is not to police language, but to ensure that lexical items be compatible with deaf experiences. The variant of LESBIAN that changes point of contact to the tip of the index finger still means "lesbian" and will have negative associations for some, but it does not identify lesbians by the act of cunnilingus; it is neither reductionist nor crude. Thus, the notion of correction must be added to discussions of language change.

The study here suggests that metalinguistic awareness can be an important component of cognitive, social, and cultural change. Changing of attitudes does not happen solely inside individual minds: people's linguistically mediated interactions collectively shape improved understandings.

6 Conclusion: What the Study of Taboo Teaches Us

We have established that taboo offers a playground for linguistic creativity in sign, just as in spoken, languages. Thus, taboo in sign languages belongs to genres that relish linguistic innovations, including humor, poetry, and storytelling (Sutton-Spence & Kaneko 2016).

Our introduction to taboo studies raises challenges for linguistic field work (in Section 1). Recognizing taboo topics particular to deaf experience can benefit linguists by giving depth to and contextualizing the environments in which sign languages are used and proliferate. Communities of hearing people that are oppressed or marginalized, and of which only a small, privileged group interacts with the majority culture, may have analogous taboos that are yet un(der)studied. Instead, studying linguistic variation within deaf communities can broaden insight into the scope of language variation generally.

We have seen that emphasis falls together with rudeness in both modalities (Section 3). Why is that? It would seem to be merely a case of strong language. When insulting or emphasizing, you want to be strong. Why not be efficient and use one mechanism, allowing context to distinguish between senses?

Given this, it is useful to consider measures of strength in language. One is how long it stays in short term memory. In surprise memory tests, recall of taboo terms and language concerning taboo topics is superior (Allan & Burridge 2006). And among facial expressions, angry ones (closely aligned to those in rude signing) have enhanced recall and superior accuracy in surprise recognition tasks when presented to depressed individuals (Wells et al. 2010). Since signers have superior working memory for faces than nonsigners and since this is centered on recall of facial features with communicative importance (eyes, mouth, nose) rather than other features (shape of the face, protrusion of the cheekbones, etc.; see Keehner and Atkinson 2006), memory could be the relevant measure for strength regarding nonmanuals, too.

Both modalities can use lexical and nonlexical features to show strength, but in a sign language the nonmanuals seem to be a necessary part of strength while in a spoken language, prosody, for example, is not always important to strength. The differences between the two modalities then is not one of spoken languages using taboo terms while sign languages use nonmanuals, but rather the extent to which each uses both mechanisms.

We suggest that the contrast between reliance on nonmanuals for rudeness or emphasis in ASL and frequent use of taboo terms for those purposes among speakers of many western spoken languages is due to timing differences between the modalities. Speech articulators move more quickly than sign articulators. Adding lexical items to a sign sentence increases its duration more than adding lexical items to a spoken sentence (Klima & Bellugi 1979). That accounts at least partially for why sign languages use layering or simultaneity (e.g., Bellugi & Fischer 1972; Wilbur 2000). Exploitation of the affective nonmanuals, in contrast to addition of lexical items, requires no additional time. Affective nonmanuals are the perfect way to convey rudeness and emphasis in sign.

We have seen that examination of bleached taboo predicates uncovered syntactic structures otherwise unnoticed (Section 3). Why is that? Is the linguistic creativity here due to the taboo-term history of these signs? Could non-taboo interjections, such as PAH! (expression of triumph), become predicates and exhibit the same range of syntactic behavior we saw with bleached taboo-term predicates or, perhaps, new syntactic behavior? In English we find such predicates (*They wowed me with that presentation*), but they don't behave uniquely. Right now our preliminary answer is no – so taboo is the key.

On the other hand, taboo terms have unusual morphological and syntactic behavior in spoken languages – such as being infixes in English (*fanfuckingtastic, fanfreakingtastic*, etc.). Such grammatically innovative uses involve nonliteral readings of the taboo terms. Likewise, the taboo terms that exhibit innovative behavior in ASL are not understood literally; they are bleached.

At this point, we tentatively but optimistically attribute the innovative character of bleached taboo predicates in ASL to both their origins in taboo and the fact that they've been bleached. When taboo terms start to lose their vulgar sense, they become the new guys on the block, and, initially, the (mildly) naughty boys. Signers can explore the limits of the grammar with them, particularly adolescents, the innovators in sign (Battison 1978) just as in spoken language (Eckert 2000). More work needs to be done on taboo terms, since this is one area of the grammar where normative influences can be expected to be minimal, so creative play can be maximal.

We have recognized a new motivation for language change: correction (Section 4). Our study concerns correction in sign languages as used by deaf communities; thus, we mentioned spoken languages only briefly. This is natural, since nonarbitrary relationships between form and sense arise more frequently in sign than spoken languages. However, in recent years many have shown that sound iconicity has extensive effect on the lexicon even in languages such as English (e.g., Waugh & Newfield 1995; Winter et al. 2017), particularly regarding objects with respect to their size (Winter & Perlman 2021), shape (Ćwiek et al. 2022), and roughness (Winter et al. 2022). And when we look outside the Indo-European family, we find many associations between phonemes and senses (e.g., Hinton, Nichols & Ohala 2006) and sound-meaning mappings dealing with "sensory, motor and affective experiences as well as aspects of the spatio-temporal unfolding of an event" (Vigliocco, Perniss & Vinson 2014: 3). We therefore might expect to find lexical corrections among spoken languages that have higher frequency of iconicity, such as those of Japan, Korea, Southeast Asia, sub-Saharan Africa, the Balto-Finnic group, the Australian Aborigines, and the Indigenous peoples of South America (Perniss, Thompson & Vigliocco 2010). If the motivations for (sub)lexical correction presented here are on the right track, we'd expect languages that have been suppressed or oppressed to show even more propensity toward corrections.

Still, deaf communities might be extreme regarding (sub)lexical correction, given the special status of language acquisition among deaf people. It may well be that pressure for correction is greater when the lexical item is at odds with perceptions of realities and truths that deaf individuals and communities hold dear.

Appendix: Handshapes Referred To

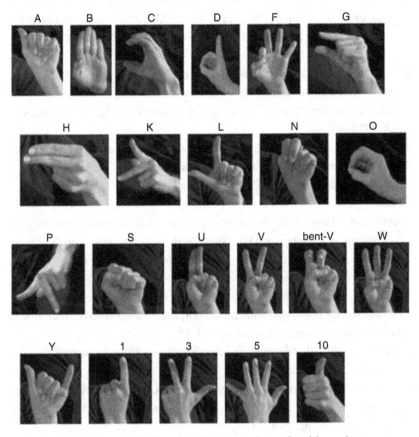

Source: www.lifeprint.com/asl101/pages-layout/handshapes.htm

References

Abelin, Å. (1999). Phonesthemes in Swedish. *Proceedings of XIV International Conference of Phonetic Sciences*, **99**, 1333–1336. www.international phoneticassociation.org/icphs-proceedings/ICPhS1999/papers/p14_1333 .pdf.

Allan, K., ed. (2018). *The Oxford handbook of taboo words and language.* Oxford: Oxford University Press. https://www .internationalphoneticassociation.org/icphs-proceedings/ICPhS1999/papers/ p14_1333.pdf

Allan, K. & Burridge, K. (2006). *Forbidden words: Taboo and the censoring of language.* Cambridge: Cambridge University Press.

Andersson, L. & Trudgill, P. (1990). *Bad language.* Oxford: Oxford University Press.

Aramburo, A. (1994). Sociolinguistic aspects of the Black deaf community. In C. J. Erting, R. C. Johnson, D. L. Smith & B. D. Snider, eds., *The Deaf way: Perspectives from the International Conference on Deaf Culture.* Washington, DC: Gallaudet University Press, pp. 474–482.

Aronoff, M., Meir, I., Padden, C. & Sandler, W. (2004). Morphological universals and the sign language type. In G. Booij & J. van Marle, eds., *Yearbook of morphology.* Dordrecht: Kluwer, pp. 19–39.

Aubrecht, A. (2017). Message of love. YouTube video. www.youtube.com /watch?v=2D78-5p3s5E.

Azzaro, G. (2018). Taboo language in books, films, and the media. In K. Allen, ed., *The Oxford handbook of taboo words and language.* Oxford: Oxford University Press, pp. 280–307.

Back, L. T., Keys, C. B., McMahon, S. D. & O'Neill, K. (2016). How we label students with disabilities: A framework of language use in an urban school district in the United States. *Disability Studies Quarterly*, **36**(4). https://doi .org/10.18061/dsq.v36i4.4387.

Badarneh, M. A. (2010). The pragmatics of diminutives in colloquial Jordanian Arabic. *Journal of Pragmatics*, **42**(1), 153–167.

Baker-Shenk, C. (1986). Characteristics of oppressed and oppressor peoples: Their effect on the interpreting context. In M. L. McIntire, ed., *Interpreting: The art of cross-cultural mediation.* Alexandria, VA: Registry of Interpreters, pp. 43–54.

Baker-Shenk, C. & Cokely, D. (1991). Transcription symbols. In *American Sign Language: A teacher's resource text on grammar and culture*. Washington, DC: Gallaudet University Press, pp. 1–29.

Bat-Chava, Y. (1994). Group identification and self-esteem of deaf adults. *Personality and Psychology Bulletin*, **20**(5), 494–502.

Battison, R. M. (1978). *Lexical borrowing in American Sign Language*. Silver Spring, MD: Linstock Press.

Battison, R. M. (2013). American Sign Language linguistics 1970–1980: Memoir of a renaissance. In K. Emmorey & H. L. Lane, eds., *The signs of language revisited*. New York: Psychology Press, pp. 17–25.

Bauman, H.-D. L., ed. (2008). *Open your eyes: Deaf studies talking*. Minneapolis: University of Minnesota Press.

Bauman, H.-D. L. (2009). Postscript: Gallaudet protests of 2006 and the myths of in/exclusion. *Sign Language Studies*, **10**(1), 90–104.

Bauman, H.-D. L., Nelson, J. L. & Rose, H. M. (2006). *Signing the body poetic: Essays on American Sign Language literature*. Berkeley: University of California Press.

Bellugi, U. & Fischer, S. (1972). A comparison of sign language and spoken language. *Cognition*, **1**(2–3), 173–200.

Benedicto, E. & Brentari, D. (2004). Where did all the arguments go? Argument-changing properties of classifiers in ASL. *Natural Language & Linguistic Theory*, **22**(4), 743–810.

Benedicto, E., Cvejanov, C. & Quer, J. (2008). The morphosyntax of verbs of motion in serial constructions: A crosslinguistic study in three signed languages. In J. Quer, ed., *Signs of the time: Selected papers from TISLR 8*. Hamburg: Signum, pp. 111–132.

Bishop, M. & Hicks, S. (2005). Orange eyes: Bimodal bilingualism in hearing adults from deaf families. *Sign Language Studies*, **5**(2), 188–230.

Blake, B. J. (2018). Taboo language as source of comedy. In K. Allen, ed., *The Oxford handbook of taboo words and language*. Oxford: Oxford University Press, pp. 353–371.

Bridges, B. & Metzger, M. (1996). *Deaf tend your: Non-manual signals in ASL*. Silver Spring, MD: Calliope Press.

Brother, M. (2017). Messages from our founder & president. www.coda-international.org/milliebrother.

Brueggemann, B. J. & Burch, S. (2006). *Women and deafness: Double visions*. Washington, DC: Gallaudet University Press.

Burch, S. (2004). *Signs of resistance: American deaf cultural history, 1900 to World War II*. New York: New York University Press.

Burch, S. & Joyner, H. (2007). *Unspeakable: The story of Junius Wilson.* Chapel Hill: University of North Carolina Press.

Burch, S. & Sutherland, I. (2006). Who's not yet here? American disability history. *Radical History Review*, **94**, 127–147.

Burdiss, C. (2016). More about the deaf grassroots movement. www .paraquad.org/blog/more-about-deaf-grassroots-movement/.

Burke, M. (2013). SPEAKOUT: Deaf or Disabled, Deaf and Disabled, or DeafDisabled? *The Buff and Blue*. www.thebuffandblue.net/?p=11156.

Burridge, K. (2012). Euphemism and language change: The sixth and seventh ages. *Journal in English Lexicography*, **7**, 65–92.

Caselli, N. K., Sehyr, Z. S., Cohen-Goldberg, A. M. & Emmorey, K. (2017). ASL-LEX: A lexical database of American Sign Language. *Behavior Research Methods*, **49**, 784–801.

Cho, S. J. & Tian, Y. (2020). Why do they keep swearing? The role of outcome expectations between descriptive norms and swearing among Korean youths: A test of the theory of normative social behavior. *Western Journal of Communication*, **84**(2), 227–244.

Cifuentes-Férez, P. & Rojo, A. (2015). Thinking for translating: A think-aloud protocol on the translation of manner-of-motion verbs. *Target: International Journal of Translation Studies*, **27**(2), 273–300.

Costello, B., Fernández, J. & Landa, A. (2006). The non-(existent) native signer: Sign language research in a small Deaf population. In R. M. de Quadros, ed., *Theoretical issues in sign language research 9*. Rio de Janeiro: Editora Arara Azul, pp. 77–94.

Coulter, G. (1990). Emphatic stress in ASL. In S. D. Fischer & P. Siple, eds., *Theoretical issues in sign language research: Linguistics*, vol 1. Chicago: University of Chicago Press, pp. 109–126.

Crenshaw, K. (1989). Demarginalizing the intersection of race and sex: A black feminist critique of antidiscrimination doctrine, feminist theory and antiracist politics. *University of Chicago Legal Forum*, **140**, 139–167.

Croce, N. E. (1985). Everyone here spoke sign language: Hereditary deafness on Martha's Vineyard. Cambridge, MA: Harvard University Press.

Cruz, R., Firestone, A. & Love, M. (2023). Beyond a seat at the table: Imagining educational equity through critical inclusion. *Educational Review*, 1–27. http://doi.org/10.1080/00131911.2023.2173726.

Culpeper, J. (2011). *Impoliteness: Using language to cause offence.* Cambridge: Cambridge University Press.

Ćwiek, A., Fuchs, S., Draxler, C. et al. (2022). The bouba/kiki effect is robust across cultures and writing systems. *Philosophical Transactions of the Royal*

Society B, **377**(1841), article 20200390. https://royalsocietypublishing.org/doi/full/10.1098/rstb.2020.0390.

Davey, S. & Phillips, J. (2013). A new challenge: The deaf-wannabe. *Clinical Otolaryngology*, **38**(1), 109–110.

Davis, L. J. (2002). Postdeafness. In H.-D. L. Bauman, ed., *Open your eyes: Deaf studies talking*. Washington, DC: Gallaudet University Press, pp. 314–326.

Davis, L. J. (2007). Deafness and the riddle of identity. *The Chronicle Review* (January 12), 1–7.

Deaf Women United (2016). Our mission: Embracing deaf womanhood through ongoing connections, advocacy and awareness. www.dwu.org/about_us.

Deal, M. (2003). Disabled people's attitudes toward other impairment groups: A hierarchy of impairments. *Disability and Society*, **18**(7), 897–910.

DiMarco, N. & Man, C. (2018). Nyle DiMarco & Chella Man teach us queer sign language. YouTube video. www.youtube.com/watch?v=8HX0HGapok.

Dressler, W. U. & Barbaresi, L. M. (2011). *Morphopragmatics: Diminutives and intensifiers in Italian, German, and other languages*. Berlin: Walter de Gruyter.

Eckert, P. (2000). *Linguistic variation as social practice*. Malden, MA: Blackwell.

Eckhardt, J. (2002). Profile: Alison Aubrecht, counselor and poet (Part 1: Identity). www.michdhh.org/profiles/aubrecht_alison.html.

Edwards, T. (2014). From compensation to integration: Effects of the pro-tactile movement on the sublexical structure of Tactile American Sign Language. *Journal of Pragmatics*, **69**, 22–41.

Edwards, T. (2018). Re-Channeling language: The mutual restructuring of language and infrastructure among DeafBlind people at Gallaudet University. *Journal of Linguistic Anthropology*, **28**(3), 273–292.

Edwards, T. (2022). The difference intersubjective grammar makes in protactile DeafBlind communities. *Lingua*, **273**, 103303.

Emmorey, K., Gertsberg, N., Korpics, F. & Wright, C. E. (2009). The influence of visual feedback and register changes on sign language production: A kinematic study with deaf signers. *Applied Psycholinguistics*, **30**, 187–203.

Fenlon, J., Denmark, T., Campbell, R. & Woll, B. (2007). Seeing sentence boundaries. *Sign Language and Linguistics*, **10**(2), 177–200.

Fine, H. & Fine, P., exec. prods. (1990). *Sixty Minutes*. New York: Columbia Broadcasting System.

Fischer, S. D. & Lillo-Martin, D. (1990). UNDERSTANDING conjunctions. *International Journal of Sign Linguistics*, **1**(2), 71–80.

Fisher, J., Mirus G. & Napoli, D.J. (2018). Sᴛɪᴄᴋʏ: Taboo topics in deaf communities. In K. Allan, ed., *The Oxford handbook of taboo words and language.* Oxford: Oxford University Press, pp. 182–213.

Flying Words Project (2008). Poetry. From *The year of walking dogs* (DVD). www.youtube.com/watch?v=JnU3U6qEibU

Fox, T. F. (1880). Social Status of the Deaf. In *Proceedings of the Second National Convention of Deaf-Mutes.* New York: New York Institution of the Deaf and Dumb, pp. 13–16.

Frishberg, N. (1975). Arbitrariness and iconicity: Historical change in American Sign Language. *Language,* **51**(3), 696–719.

Garberoglio, C., Johnson, P., Sales, A. & Cawthon, S. W. (2021). Change over time in educational attainment for deaf individuals from 2008–2018. *Journal of Postsecondary Education and Disability,* **34**(3), 253–272.

Galvin, R. (2003). The making of the disabled identity: A linguistic analysis of marginalisation. *Disability Studies Quarterly,* **23**(2), 149–178.

Gawinkowska, M., Paradowski, M. B. & Bilewicz, M. (2013). Second language as an exemptor from sociocultural norms: Emotion-related language choice revisited. *PloS one,* **8**(12), article e81225.

George, J. E. (2011). Politeness in Japanese Sign Language (JSL): Polite JSL expression as evidence for intermodal language contact influence. Unpublished PhD thesis, University of California at Berkeley.

Grayson, G. (2003). *Talking with your hands, listening with your eyes: A complete photographic guide to American Sign Language.* Garden City Park, NY: Square One Publishers.

Greene, D. (2011). ASL for ɢᴀʏ, ʟᴇsʙɪᴀɴ, ʙɪsᴇxᴜᴀʟ ᴛʀᴀɴsɢᴇɴᴅᴇʀ, ǫᴜᴇsᴛɪᴏɴɪɴɢ. YouTube video. www.youtube.com/watch?v=jTdCZ9i1WY8.

Gregory, S. (1998). Mathematics and deaf children. In S. Gregory, P. Knight, W. McCracken, S. Powers & L. Watson, eds., *Issues in deaf education.* Abingdon: David Fulton Publishers, pp. 119–126.

Hairston, E. & Smith, L. (1983). *Black and Deaf in America.* Silver Spring, MD: TJ Publishers.

Halmari, H. (2011). Political correctness, euphemism, and language change: The case of "people first." *Journal of Pragmatics,* **43**(3), 828–840.

Hansen, S. J., McMahon, K. L. & de Zubicaray, G. I. (2019). The neurobiology of taboo language processing: fMRI evidence during spoken word production. *Social Cognitive and Affective Neuroscience,* **14**(3), 271–279.

Harris, R., Holmes, H. & Mertens, D. (2009). Research ethics in sign language communities. *Sign Language Studies,* **9**(2), 104–131.

Herrmann, A. & Steinbach, M., eds. (2013). *Nonmanuals in sign language.* Amsterdam: John Benjamins.

Hill, J. (2014). Junk Spanish, cover racism, and the (leaky) boundary between public and private spheres. *Pragmatics*, **5**(2), 197–212.

Hinton, L., Nichols, J. & Ohala, J. J., eds. (2006). *Sound symbolism*. Cambridge: Cambridge University Press.

Hochgesang, J. A. & Miller, M. T. (2016). A celebration of the *Dictionary of American Sign Language on linguistic principles*: Fifty years later. *Sign Language Studies*, **16**(4), 563–591.

Hoeksema, J. (2012). Elative compounds in Dutch: Properties and developments. In G. Oebel, ed.,*Intensivierungskonzepte bei Adjektiven und Adverben im Sprachenvergleich/Crosslinguistic comparison of intensified adjectives and adverbs*. Hamburg: Verlag dr. Kovać, pp. 97–142.

Hoeksema, J. & Napoli, D. J. (2008). Just for the hell of it: A comparison to two taboo-term constructions. *Journal of Linguistics*, **44**, 347–378.

Hoeksema, J. & Napoli, D. J. (2019). Degree resultatives as second-order constructions. *Journal of Germanic Linguistics*, **31**(3), 225–297.

Holcomb, T. (2013). *Introduction to American deaf culture*. Oxford: Oxford University Press.

Hollins, K. (2000). Between two worlds: The social implications of cochlear implantation for children born deaf. In J. Hubert, ed., *Madness, disability and social exclusion: The archaeology and anthropology of difference*. Abingdon: Routledge, pp. 180–195.

Horejes, T. P. (2012). *Social constructions of deafness: Examining deaf languacultures in education*. Washington, DC: Gallaudet University Press.

Hott, L. & Garey, D., dirs. (2007). *Through Deaf eyes*. DVD. USA: Florentine Films/Hott Productions.

Hoza, J. (2007). *It's not what you sign: It's how you sign it*. Washington, DC: Gallaudet University Press.

Hoza, J. (2008). Five nonmanual modifiers that mitigate requests and rejections in American Sign Language. *Sign Language Studies*, **8**, 264–288.

Hudnall, W. B. (1976). A study of the "grassroots" deaf community in relation to deaf advocacy. Unpublished MA thesis, California State University at Northridge.

Hughes, G. (2015). *An encyclopedia of swearing: The social history of oaths, profanity, foul language, and ethnic slurs in the English-speaking world*. Abingdon: Routledge.

Humphries, T. (1975). *Audism: The making of a word*. Unpublished manuscript. San Diego: University of California at San Diego.

Humphries, T. (1977). *Communicating across cultures (deaf/hearing) and language learning*. Unpublished PhD thesis, Union Institute, Cincinnati, OH.

Humphries, T., Kushalnagar, P., Mathur, G. et al. (2012). Language acquisition for deaf children: Reducing the harms of zero tolerance to the use of alternative approaches. *Harm Reduction Journal*, **9**(1), article 16.

Humphries, T., Kushalnagar, P., Mathur, G. et al. (2017). Discourses of prejudice in the professions: The case of sign languages. *Journal of Medical Ethics*, **43**(9), 648–652.

Janssen, M. J., Riksen-Walraven, J. M. & van Dijk, J. (2002). Enhancing the quality of interaction between deafblind children and their educators. *Journal of Developmental and Physical Disabilities*, **14**(1), 87–109.

Jay, T. (2009). The utility and ubiquity of taboo words. *Perspectives on Psychological Science*, **4**(2), 153–161.

Job, J. (2004). Factors involved in the ineffective dissemination of sexuality information to individuals who are deaf or hard of hearing. *American Annals of the Deaf*, **149**(3), 264–273.

Johnston, T. & Ferrara, L. (2012). Lexicalization in signed languages: When is an idiom not an idiom? *Selected papers from UK-CLA Meetings*, **1**, 229–248.

Johnston, T. & Schembri, A. (2007). *Australian Sign Language: An introduction to sign language linguistics*. Cambridge: Cambridge University Press.

Keehner, M., Atkinson, J. (2006). Working memory and deafness: Implications for cognitive development and functioning. In S. Pickering, ed., *Working memory and education*. London: Elsevier, pp. 189–219.

Kensicki, L. J. (2001). Deaf president now! Positive media framing of a social movement within a hegemonic political environment. *Journal of Communication Inquiry*, **25**(2), 147–166.

Kersten-Parrish, S. (2021). De-Masking deafness: Unlearning and reteaching disability during a pandemic. *Disability Studies Quarterly*, **41**(3). https://dsq-sds.org/article/view/8329/6185.

Kleinfeld, M. S. & Warner, N. (1996). Variation in the deaf community: Gay, lesbian, and bisexual signs. In C. Lucas, ed., *Multicultural aspects of sociolinguistics in deaf communities*. Washington, DC: Gallaudet University Press, pp. 3–35.

Klima, E. & Bellugi, U. (1975). Wit and poetry in American Sign Language. *Sign Language Studies*, **8**, 203–224.

Klima, E. & Bellugi, U. (1979). *The signs of language*. Cambridge, MA: Harvard University Press.

Knooihuizen, R. (2008). Fishing for words: The taboo language of Shetland fishermen and the dating of Norn language death 1. *Transactions of the Philological Society*, **106**(1), 100–113.

Kobayashi, Y. & Osugi, Y. (2020). Deaf women's participation, movements, and rights: Learning from the experiences of deaf women in Japan. *Deaf*

Studies Digital Journal, **5**. https://quod.lib.umich.edu/d/dsdj/images/ 15499139.0005.007-transcript.pdf.

Krieger, J. (2007). Grassroots: Carriers of our ASL? http://seesay-jay.blogspot.com/2007/04/grassroots-carriers-of-our-asl.html.

Künzli, A. (2009). Think-aloud protocols–A useful tool for investigating the linguistic aspect of translation. *Meta: journal des traducteurs/Meta: Translators' Journal*, **54**(2), 326–341.

Labov, T. (1992). Social and language boundaries among adolescents. *American Speech*, **67**, 339–366.

Lackner, A. (2017) *Functions of head and body movements in Austrian Sign Language*. Berlin: De Gruyter Mouton.

Lancker, D. & Cummings, J. L. (1999). Expletives: Neurolinguistic and neurobehavioral perspectives on swearing. *Brain Research Reviews*, **31**, 8–104.

Lane, H., (2002). Do deaf people have a disability? *Sign Language Studies*, **2**(4), 356–379.

Lane, H. (2005). Ethnicity, ethics, and the deaf-world. *Journal of deaf studies and deaf education*, **10**(3), 291–310.

Lane, H., Pillard, R. & French, M. (2000). Origins of the American Deaf-World: Assimilating and differentiating societies and their relation to genetic patterning. *Sign Language Studies*, **1**(1), 17–44.

Leigh, I. W. (2009). *A lens on deaf identities*. Oxford: Oxford University Press.

Leigh, I. W., Andrews, J. F. & Harris, R. (2016). *Deaf culture: Exploring deaf communities in the United States*. San Diego: Plural Publishing.

Lentz, E. M. (2014). Deafhood and deaf culture: The relationship. YouTube video. www.youtube.com/watch?v=VAKGmnhzebQ.

Lewis, K. B. & Henderson, R. (1997). *Sign language made simple*. New York: Doubleday.

Liddell, S. K. (2003). *Grammar, gesture, and meaning in American Sign Language*. Cambridge: Cambridge University Press.

Liddell, S. K. & Johnson, R. E. (1986). American Sign Language compound formation processes, lexicalization, and phonological remnants. *Natural Language & Linguistic Theory*, **4**(4), 445–513.

Liddell, S. K. & Johnson, R. E. (1989). American Sign Language: The phonological base. *Sign Language Studies*, **64**, 195–277.

Lillo-Martin, D. (1991). *Universal Grammar and American Sign Language: Setting the null argument parameters*. Dordrecht: Kluwer.

Linfoot-Ham, Kerry (2005). The linguistics of euphemism: A diachronic study of euphemism formation. *Journal of Language and Linguistics*, **4**(2), 227–263.

Llisterri, J. (1992). Speaking styles in speech research: ELSNET/ ESCA/ SALT Workshop on Integrating Speech and Natural Language. Dublin, Ireland, 15–17 July 1992. http://liceu.uab.cat/~joaquim/publicacions/SpeakingStyles_92 .pdf.

Lockwood, W. B. (1955). Word taboo in the language of the Faroese fishermen. *Transactions of the Philological Society*, **54**(1),1–24.

Longmore, P. K. & Umansky, L. (2001). *The new disability history: American perspectives*. New York: New York University Press.

Loos, C., Cramer, J. M. & Napoli, D. J. (2020). The linguistic sources of offense of taboo terms in German Sign Language. *Cognitive linguistics*, **31**(1), 73–112.

Lucas, C., Bayley, R., Rose, M. & Wulf, A. (2002). Location variation in American Sign Language. *Sign Language Studies*, **2**(4), 407–440.

Magazzù, G. (2018). Non-professional subtitling in Italy: The challenges of translating humour and taboo language. *Hikma*, **17**, 75–93.

Mandel, M. (1981). Phonotactics and morphophonology in American Sign Language. Unpublished PhD thesis, University of California, Berkeley.

Mathur, G. & Rathmann, C. (2006). Variability in verbal agreement forms across four signed languages. In L. Goldstein, D. Whalen & C. Best, eds., *Laboratory Phonology 8*. Berlin: Mouton de Gruyter, pp. 289–316.

Mathur, G. & Rathmann, C. (2010). Verb agreement in sign language morphology. In D. Brentari, ed., *Sign languages: A Cambridge language survey*. Cambridge: Cambridge University Press, pp. 173–196.

Mauldin, L. (2016). *Made to hear: Cochlear implants and raising deaf children*. Minneapolis: University of Minnesota Press.

McCaskill, C., Lucas, C., Bayley, R. & Hill, J. (2011). *The hidden treasure of Black ASL: Its history and structure*. Washington, DC: Gallaudet University Press.

McGlone, M. S., Beck, G. & Pfiester, A. (2006). Contamination and camouflage in euphemisms. *Communication Monographs*, **73**(3), 261–282.

Meir, I., Padden, C., Aronoff, M. & Sandler, W. (2007). Body as subject. *Journal of Linguistics*, **43**, 531–563.

Mesch, J. (2000). Tactile Swedish Sign Language: Turn taking in signed conversations of people who are deaf and blind. https://digitalcommons .wou.edu/dbi_culture/15

Mesch, J. & Raanes, E. (2023). Meaning-making in tactile cross-signing context. *Journal of Pragmatics*, **205**, 137–150.

Miller, R. H. (2004). *Deaf hearing boy: A memoir*. Washington, DC: Gallaudet University Press.

Mindess, A. (2006). *Reading between the signs: Intercultural communication for sign language interpreters*. Boston: Intercultural Press.

Mirus, G. (2008). *On the linguistic repertoire of Deaf cuers*. Unpublished PhD thesis, University of Texas at Austin.

Mirus, G., Fisher, J. & Napoli, D. J. (2012). Taboo expressions in American Sign Language. *Lingua*, **122**(9), 1004–1020.

Mirus, G., Fisher, J. & Napoli, D. J. (2020). (Sub) lexical changes in iconic signs to realign with community sensibilities and experiences. *Language in Society*, **49**(2), 283–309.

Mirus, G., Rathmann, C. & Meier, R. (2001). Proximalizaion and distalization of sign movement in adult learners. In V. Dively, M. Metzger, S. Taub & A. M. Baer, eds., *Signed languages: Discoveries from international research*. Washington, DC: Gallaudet University Press, pp. 103–119.

Mitchell, R. & Karchmer, M. (2004). Chasing the mythical ten percent: Parental hearing status of deaf and hard of hearing students in the United States. *Sign Language Studies*, **4**(2), 138–163.

Montagu, A. (1967). The anatomy of swearing. New York: Rapp & Whiting.

Moores, D. (2001). *Educating the Deaf: Psychology, principles, and practices*. Boston: Houghton Mifflin.

Moser, M. G. (1990). The regularity hypothesis applied to ASL. In C. Lucas, ed., *Sign language research: Theoretical issues*. Washington, DC: Gallaudet University Press, pp. 50–56.

Muansuwan, N. (2001). Directional serial verb constructions in Thai. In D. Flickinger & A. Kathol, eds., *Proceedings of the 7th International HPSG Conference, UC Berkeley (22–23 July, 2000)*. Stanford: CSLI Publications, pp. 229–246.

Muredda, A. (2012). Fixing language: "People-first" language, taxonomical prescriptivism, and the linguistic location of disability. *The English Languages: History, Diaspora, Culture*, **3**(1), 1–10.

Musselman, C. (2000). How do children who can't hear learn to read an alphabetic script? A review of the literature on reading and feafness. *Journal of Deaf Studies and Deaf Education*, **5**, 9–31.

Napoli, D. J., Fisher, J. & Mirus, G. (2013) Bleached taboo-term predicates in American Sign Language. *Lingua*, **123**, 148–167.

Napoli, D. J. & Hoeksema, J. (2009). The grammatical versatility of taboo terms. *Studies in Language*, **33**(3), 612–643.

Napoli, D. J. & Mirus, G. (2015). Shared reading activities: a recommendation for deaf children. *Global Journal of Special Education and Services*, **3**(1), 38–42.

Napoli, D. J. & Sutton-Spence, R. (2021). Clause-initial Vs in sign languages: Scene-setters. In V. Lee-Schoenfeld & D. Ott, eds., *Parameters of predicate fronting: Cross-linguistic explorations of V(P)-initial clauses.* Oxford: Oxford University Press, pp. 192–219.

Napoli, D. J., Fisher, J. & Mirus, G. (2013). Bleached taboo-term predicates in American Sign Language. *Lingua*, **123**, 148–167.

Napoli, D. J., Spence, R. S. & de Quadros, R. M. (2017). Influence of predicate sense on word order in sign languages: Intensional and extensional verbs. *Language*, **93**(3), 641–670.

Neidle, C., Opoku, A. & Metaxas, D. (2022). ASL video corpora & sign bank: Resources available through the American sign language linguistic research project (ASLLRP). *arXiv preprint arXiv:2201.07899v1* [cs.CL]. https://doi .org/10.48550/arXiv.2201.07899.

Neidle, C., Kegl, J., MacLaughlin, D., Bahan, B. & Lee, R. (2000). *The syntax of American Sign Language: Functional categories and hierarchical structure.* Cambridge, MA: MIT Press.

Nespor, M. & Sandler, W. (1999). Prosody in Israeli Sign Language. *Language and Speech*, **42**(2–3), 143–176.

Nicodemus, B. (2009). *Prosodic markers and utterance boundaries in American Sign Language interpretation.* Washington, DC: Gallaudet University Press.

O'Connell, N. P. (2016). A tale of two schools: Educating Catholic female deaf children in Ireland, 1846–1946. *History of Education*, **45**(2), 188–205.

O'Driscoll, J. (2020). *Offensive language: Taboo, offence and social control.* New York: Bloomsbury Publishing.

Ormel, E. & Crasborn, O. (2012). Prosodic correlates of sentences in signed languages. *Sign Language Studies*, **12**(2), 109–145.

Padden, C. (1988). *Interaction of morphology and syntax in American Sign Language.* New York: Garland Press.

Padden, C. & Humphries, T. (1988). *Deaf in America: Voices from a culture.* Cambridge, MA: Harvard University Press.

Padden, C. & Perlmutter, D. (1987). American Sign Language and the architecture of phonological theory. *Natural Language and Linguistic Theory*, **5**, 335–375.

Pendzich, N.-K. (2020). *Lexical nonmanuals in German Sign Language.* Berlin: De Gruyter Mouton.

Pénicaud, S., Klein, D., Zatorre, R. J. et al. (2013). Structural brain changes linked to delayed first language acquisition in congenitally deaf individuals. *NeuroImage*, **66**(1), 42–49.

Permenter, C. (2012). Deaf community outraged by dirty sign language book. www.lackuna.com/2012/07/02/deaf-community-outraged-by-dirty-sign-language-book/

Perniss, P., Thompson, R. L. & Vigliocco, G. (2010). Iconicity as a general property of language: Evidence from spoken and signed languages. *Frontiers in Psychology*, **1**. http://doi.org/10.3389/fpsyg.2010.00227.

Petitto, L. A., Zatorre, R. A., Gauna, K. et al. (2000). Speech-like cerebral activity in profoundly deaf people processing signed languages: Implications for the neural basis of human language. *Proceedings of the National Academy of Science*, **97**(25), 13961–13966.

Petronio, K. (1993). Clause structure in American Sign Language. Unpublished PhD thesis, University of Washington.

Pfau, R. & Quer, J. (2010). Nonmanuals: Their grammatical and prosodic roles. In D. Brentari, ed., *Sign languages*. Cambridge: Cambridge University Press, pp. 381–402.

Pfau, R. & Steinbach, M. (2006). Pluralization in sign and in speech: A cross-modal typological study. *Linguistic Typology*, **10**, 135–182.

Pfau, R., Salzmann, M. & Steinbach, M. (2018). The syntax of sign language agreement: Common ingredients, but unusual recipe. *Glossa: A Journal of General Linguistics*, **3**(1), article 107. http://doi.org/10.5334/gjgl.511

Pietrosemoli, L. (1994). Sign terminology for sex and death in Venezuelan deaf and hearing cultures: A preliminary study of pragmatic interference. In C. Erting, R. C. Johnson, D. L. Smith & B. D. Snider, eds., *The deaf way*. Washington, DC: Gallaudet University Press, pp. 677–683.

Pilotti, M., Almand, J., Mahamane, S. & Martinez, M. (2012). Taboo words in expressive language: Do sex and primary language matter. *American International Journal of Contemporary Research*, **2**(2), 17–26.

Pizzuto, E. & Corazza, S. (1996). Noun morphology in Italian Sign Language (LIS). *Lingua*, **98**(1–3), 169–196.

Powell, A. (2012). Deaf community rallies against Dirty Signs with Kristin. *The Daily Dot*. www.dailydot.com/news/deaf-community-petition-dirty-signs-kristin/.

Preston, P. (1994). *Mother father deaf: Living between sound and silence*. Cambridge, MA: Harvard University Press.

Project-Easier. 2021. Overview of datasets for the sign languages of Europe. www.project-easier.eu/wp-content/uploads/sites/67/2021/08/EASIER-D6.1-Overview-of-Datasets-for-the-Sign-Languages-of-Europe.pdf.

Pyers, J. (2006). Indicating the body: Expression of body part terminology in American Sign Language. *Language Sciences*, **28**(2–3), 280–303.

84 *References*

Quinto-Pozos, D. & Adam, R. (2015). Sign languages in contact. In A. C. Schembri and C. Lucas, eds., *Sociolinguistics and deaf communities*. Cambridge: Cambridge University Press, pp. 29–60.

Robinson, C. L. (2006). Visual screaming: Willy Conley's deaf theatre and Charlie Chaplin's silent cinema. In H.-D. L. Bauman, J. L. Nelson & H. M. Rose, eds., *Signing the body poetic: Essays on American Sign Language literature*. Berkeley: University of California Press, pp. 195–215.

Robinson, O. E. (2010). We are a different class: Ableist rhetoric in Deaf America, 1880-1920. In S. Burch and A. Kafer, eds., *Deaf and disability studies*. Washington, DC: Gallaudet University Press, pp. 5–21.

Robinson, O. E. (2012). The Deaf do not beg: Making the case for citizenship, 1880–1956. Unpublished PhD thesis, The Ohio State University.

Roush, D. (2007). Indirectness strategies in American Sign Language requests and refusals: Deconstructing the Deaf-as-direct stereotype. In M. Metzger and E. Fleetwood, eds., *Translation, sociolinguistic, and consumer issues in interpreting*. Washington, DC: Gallaudet University Press, pp. 103–158.

Rudner, W. A. & Butowsky. R. (1981). Signs used in the deaf gay community. *Sign Language Studies*, **30**(1), 36–48.

Rush, C. (2014). From the mouth of a hard-of-hearing student. August 29. http://silentethnography.blogspot.com/.

Rutherford, S. (1993). *A study of American Deaf folklore*. Burtonsville, MD: Linstok Press.

Sandler, W. & Lillo-Martin, D. (2006). *Sign language and linguistic universals*. Cambridge: Cambridge University Press.

Saunders, K. C. (2016). A double-edged sword: Social media as a tool of online disinhibition regarding American Sign Language and Deaf Cultural experience marginalization, and as a tool of cultural and linguistic exposure. *Social Media + Society*, **2**(1). doi: 10.1177/2056305115624529.

Schein J. D. (1989). *At home among strangers*. Washington, DC: Gallaudet University Press.

Schein, J. & Stewart, D. (1995). *Language in motion: Exploring the nature of sign*. Washington, DC: Gallaudet University Press.

Seliger, S. (2012). Why won't they get hearing aids? *New York Times*. https://newoldage.blogs.nytimes.com/2012/04/05/why-wont-they-get-hearing-aids/.

Schwager, W. & Zeshan, U. (2008). Word classes in sign languages. *Studies in Language*, **32**(3), 509–545.

Shaffer, B. (2004). Information ordering and speaker subjectivity: Modality in ASL. *Cognitive Linguistics*, **15**(2), 175–195.

Shannon, Rogan (2017). Queer signs. YouTube video. www.youtube.com/watch?v=KfPAkVGWtMY.

Sheridan, M. A. (2001). Deaf women now: Establishing our niche. In L. Bragg, ed., *Deaf World: A historical reader and primary sourcebook.* New York: New York University Press, pp. 380–389.

SignSchool (2016a). COME-OUT. YouTube video. www.youtube.com/watch? v=TXQ3WpRIUDg.

SignSchool (2016b). COME-OUT-OF-THE-CLOSET. YouTube video. www .youtube.com/watch?time_continue=1&v=88iTOlH7XYQ

Singleton, J. L., Jones, G. & Hanumantha, S. (2014). Toward ethical research practice with Deaf participants. *Journal of Empirical Research on Human Research Ethics,* **9**, 59–66.

Singleton, J. L., Martin, A. J. & Morgan, G. (2015). Ethics, Deaf-friendly research, and good practice when studying sign languages. In E. Orfanidou, B. Woll & G. Morgan, eds.,*Research methods in sign language studies: A practical guide.* Hoboken, NJ: Wiley-Blackwell, pp. 7–20.

Solomon, A. (2012). *Far from the tree: Parents, children and the search for identity.* New York: Simon & Schuster.

Solomon, C. & Miller, J. A. (2014). Sign language is not performance art. *The Baltimore Sun.* April 26. http://articles.baltimoresun.com/2014-04-25/news/ bs-ed-media-and-sign-language-20140426_1_american-sign-language-deaf -americans-deaf-people.

Song, S., Zilverstand, A., Song, H. et al. (2017). The influence of emotional interference on cognitive control: A meta-analysis of neuroimaging studies using the emotional Stroop task. *Scientific Reports,* **7**(1), 1–9.

Start ASL. (2008-2017). Famous deaf people. www.startasl.com/famous-deaf-people_html.

Stauffer, L. K. (2012). ASL students' ability to self assess ASL competency. *Journal of Interpretation,* **21**(1), 79–90.

Stokoe, W. C., Bernard, H. R. & Padden, C. (1976). An elite group in deaf society. *Sign Language Studies,* **12**, 189–210.

Stone, C. (2009). *Toward a deaf translation norm.* Washington, DC: Gallaudet University Press.

Suggs, T. (2012). A deaf perspective: Cultural respect in sign language inter-preting. *Street Leverage.* www.streetleverage.com/2012/08/a-deaf-perspective-cultural-respect-in-sign-language-interpreting/.

Supalla, S. (1992). *The book of name signs: Naming in American Sign Language.* San Diego: Dawn Sign Press.

Supalla, T. & Newport, E. (1978). How many seats in a chair? The derivation of nouns and verbs in American Sign Language. In P. Siple, ed., *Understanding language through sign language research.* New York: Academic Press, pp. 91–32.

Sutton-Spence, R. & Boyes Braem, P. (2013). Comparing the products and the processes of creating sign language poetry and pantomimic improvisations. *Journal of Nonverbal Behavior*, **37**(4), 245–280.

Sutton-Spence, R. & Kaneko, M. (2016). *Introducing sign language literature: Folklore and creativity*. New York: Palgrave.

Sutton-Spence, R. & Napoli. D. J. (2009). *Humour in sign languages: The linguistic underpinnings*. Dublin: Trinity College.

Sutton-Spence, R. & Woll, B. (1999). *The linguistics of British Sign Language: An introduction*. Cambridge: Cambridge University Press.

Swinbourne, C. (2013). The 10 annoying habits of hearing people. http://limpingchicken.com/2013/05/20/charlie-swinbourne-the-10-incredibly-annoying-habits-of-hearing-people/.

Sze, F. Y. B., Wei, M. X. & Wong, A. Y. L. (2017). Taboos and euphemisms in sex-related signs in Asian sign languages. *Linguistics*, **55**(1), 153–205.

Tang, G., Brentari, D., González, C. & Sze, F. (2010). Crosslinguistic variation in the use of prosodic cues: The case of blinks. In D. Brentari, ed.,*Sign languages*. Cambridge: Cambridge University Press, pp. 519–542.

Taylor, M. (2017). Deaf people teach us bad words in sign language. YouTube video. www.youtube.com/watch?v=pdOU3czs-NY&ab_channel=WatchCutVideo

Tierney, J. D. (2017). The laughing truth: Race and humor in a documentary filmmaking class. *Knowledge Cultures*, **5**(3), 38–46.

Tropp, L. R. & Wright, S. C. (2001). Ingroup identification as the inclusion of ingroup in the self. *Personality and Social Psychology Bulletin*, **27**(5), 585–600.

TrueBizMe. (2012). Update: Action alert: Hearing person exploiting ASL for profit. https://truebizme.wordpress.com/2012/06/28/action-alert-hearing-person-exploiting-asl-for-profit/

Van Oudenhoven, J. P., de Raad, B., Askevis-Leherpeux, F. et al. (2008). Terms of abuse as expression and reinforcement of cultures. *International Journal of Intercultural Relations*, **32**(2), 174–185.

van Someren, M. W., Barnard, Y. F. & Sandberg, J. A. C. (1994). *The think aloud method: A practical guide to modeling cognitive processes*. San Diego: Academic Press.

Veale, D. (2006). A compelling desire for deafness. *Journal of Deaf Studies and Deaf Education*, **11**(3), 369–372.

Vigliocco, G., Perniss, P. & Vinson, D. (2014). Language as a multimodal phenomenon: Implications for language learning, processing and evolution. *Philosophical Transactions of the Royal Society B: Biological Sciences*, **369**. http://doi.org/10.1098/rstb.2013.0292.

Voghel, A. (2005). Phonologically identical noun-verb pairs in Quebec Sign Language (LSQ): Form and context. *Toronto Working Papers in Linguistics*, **25**, 68–75.

Waugh, L. R. & Newfield, N. (1995). Iconicity in the lexicon and its relevance for a theory of morphology. In M. E. Landsberg, ed., *Syntactic Iconicity and Linguistic Freezes: The Human Dimension*. Berlin: Mouton de Gruyter, pp. 189–221.

Wells, T., Beevers, C., Robison, A. & Ellis, A. (2010). Gaze behavior predicts memory bias for angry facial expressions in stable dysphoria. *Emotion*, **10**(6), 894–902.

Wilbur, R. B. (1987). *American Sign Language: Linguistic and applied dimensions*. Boston: College-Hill.

Wilbur, R. B. (1996). Evidence for the function and structure of Wh-clefts in American Sign Language. *International Review of Sign Linguistics*, **22**, 209–256.

Wilbur, R. (2000). Phonological and prosodic layering of nonmanuals in American Sign Language. In K. Emmorey & H. Lane, eds., *The signs of language revisited: An anthology to honor Ursula Bellugi and Edward Klima*. Mahwah, NJ: Lawrence Erlbaum, pp. 190–214.

Wilbur, R. B. (2005). A reanalysis of reduplication in American Sign Language. In B. Hurch, ed., *Studies in Reduplication*. Berlin: Mouton de Gruyter, pp. 593–620.

Wilbur, R. B. (2011). Modality and the structure of sign language: Sign languages versus signed systems. In M. Marschark and P. E. Spencer, eds., *Oxford handbook of deaf studies, language, and education*, 2nd ed. Oxford: Oxford University Press, pp. 350–366.

Wilbur, R. B. (2016). Preference for clause order in complex sentences with adverbial clauses in American Sign Language. In R. Pfau, M. Steinbach & A. Herrmann, eds., *A matter of complexity: Subordination in sign languages*. Berlin: De Gruyter Mouton, pp. 36–64.

Wilbur, R. & Martínez, A. (2002). Physical correlates of prosodic structure in American Sign Language. *CLS*, **38**(1), 693–704.

Wilbur, R. & Patschke, C. (1999). Syntactic correlates of brow raise in ASL. *Sign Language and Linguistics*, **2**, 3–41.

Wilcox, P. (2000). *Metaphor in American Sign Language*. Washington, DC: Gallaudet University Press.

Wilcox, S. (2009). Symbol and symptom: Routes from gesture to sign language. *Second Annual Review of Cognitive Linguistics*, **7**(1), 89–110.

Wilson, R. (2013). Another language is another soul. *Language and Intercultural Communication*, **13**(3), pp. 298–309.

Winter, B. & Perlman, M. (2021). Size sound symbolism in the English lexicon. *Glossa: A Journal of General Linguistics*, **6**(1), article 79. https://doi.org/10.5334/gjgl.1646.

Winter, B., Perlman, M., Perry, L. K. & Lupyan, G. (2017). Which words are most iconic? Iconicity in English sensory words. *Interaction Studies*, **18**(3), 443–464.

Winter, B., Sóskuthy, M., Perlman, M. & Dingemanse, M. (2022). Trilled/r/is associated with roughness, linking sound and touch across spoken languages. *Scientific Reports*, **12**(1), article 1035. https://www.nature.com/articles/s41598-021-04311-7

Winter, W. (1970). Basic principles of the comparative method. In P. L. Gavin, ed., *Method and theory in linguistics*. Berlin: De Gruyter Mouton, pp. 147–156.

Wood, S. K. (1999). Semantic and syntactic aspects of negation in ASL. Unpublished MA thesis, Purdue University.

Woodward, J. (1979). *Signs of sexual behavior: An introduction to some sex-related vocabulary in American Sign Language*. Silver Spring, MD: T. J. Publishers.

Zola, C. (2015). Let's talk (or sign!) about the deaf, not hearing interpreters. www.slate.com/blogs/lexicon_valley/2015/06/10/sign_language_let_s_talk_or_sign_about_the_deaf_not_hearing_interpreters.html.

Zorc, R. D. (1990). The Austronesian monosyllabic root, radical or pho-nestheme. In P. Baldi, ed., *Linguistic change and reconstruction methodology*. Berlin: De Gruyter Mouton, pp. 175–194.

Acknowledgements

For Sections 3 and 4, we thank Rachel Sutton-Spence for comments on an early draft. We thank Rosanna Kim and Becky Wright for bringing to our attention certain insulting name signs. We thank Paulette, Randy, Dan, and Matthew Fisher, Erin Kearney Fisher, Alicia McClurkan, and Rosanna Kim for discussing data with us on multiple occasions.

For Section 4, we thank Daniel Altshuler, Jack Hoeksema, Jason Kandybowicz, Vera Lee-Schoenfeld, Gaurav Mathur, and Carol Padden for comments on an early draft. We thank the Long Room Hub at Trinity College Dublin for giving a fellowship to one of our authors, enabling part of this work. We thank our anonymous reviewers, who gave us examples and citations, not just criticisms and comments.

For Section 5, we thank Julie Hochgesang, Sally McConnell-Ginet, and Ceil Lucas for discussions of various points in an early draft.

For comments throughout we thank our anonymous reviewers for helping organize our materials and sharpen our arguments, and sometimes even supplying data.

We thank the original journal editors for their patience and encouragement, and, finally, we thank the editors of this elements series, Erin Wilkinson and David Quinto-Pozos, for guiding us through the whole process with thoughtful feedback and with abiding kindness.

Cambridge Elements ⁼

Sign Languages

Erin Wilkinson

University of New Mexico

Erin Wilkinson is Associate Professor in the Department of Linguistics at the University of New Mexico. She has broad research interests in bilingualism and multilingualism, language documentation and description, language change and variation, signed language typology, and language planning and policy in highly diverse signing communities. Her current studies in collaboration with other researchers examine cognitive and linguistic processing in signing bilingual populations. She also explores what linguistic structures are re-structured over time in signed languages and what are possible factors that contribute to language change and variation in signed languages in the lens of usage-based theory.

David Quinto-Pozos

University of Texas at Austin

David Quinto-Pozos is an Associate Professor in the Department of Linguistics at the University of Texas at Austin. His research interests include signed language contact and change, the interaction of language and gesture, L1 and L2 signed language acquisition, spoken-signed language interpretation, and vocabulary knowledge and literacy. He has served as an editor/co-editor of four volumes on signed language research, including *Modality and Structure in Signed and Spoken Languages* (Meier, Cormier & Quinto-Pozos, eds. 2002; Cambridge University Press), *Sign Languages in Contact* (Quinto-Pozos, ed. 2007; Gallaudet University Press), *Multilingual Aspects of Signed Language Communication and Disorder* (Quinto-Pozos, 2014; Multilingual Matters), and *Toward Effective Practice: Interpreting in Spanish-influenced Settings* (Annarino, Aponte-Samalot & Quinto-Pozos, 2014; National Consortium of Interpreter Education Centers).

About the Series

This Elements series covers a broad range of topics on signed language structure and use, describing dozens of different signed languages, along with accounts of signing (deaf and non-deaf) communities. The series is accessible (via print, electronic media, and video-based summaries) to a large deaf/signing-friendly audience.

Cambridge Elements ≡

Sign Languages

Elements in the Series

A Family-Centered Signed Language Curriculum to Support Deaf Children's Language Acquisition
Razi M. Zarchy and Leah C. Geer

Creative Sign Language
Rachel Sutton-Spence and Fernanda de Araújo Machado

Taboo in Sign Languages
Donna Jo Napoli, Jami Fisher and Gene Mirus

A full series listing is available at: www.cambridge.org/EISL

Printed in the United States
by Baker & Taylor Publisher Services